THE
PARENTS' GUIDE
TO STUDYING
AND LEARNING

**Practical strategies, tips, and tools to
support your student's success**

High School Edition

THE PARENTS' GUIDE TO STUDYING AND LEARNING

Practical strategies, tips, and tools to support your student's success

High School Edition

Saundra Yancy McGuire, PhD
with Stephanie McGuire, PhD

WISE**ACTION**

As a companion to this book,
more than 50 handouts to
support your students are available
at **www.studyandlearn.guide**.

To register and download,
use purchase code **PGSL2022**.

WISE**ACTION**

Wise Action
201 N. Union Street, Suite 110
Alexandria, Virginia 22301
https://wiseaction.co

First Wise Action trade paperback edition January 2022

Wise Action and design are trademarks of Wise Action Company.

Bulk purchase special discounts are available. Please make inquiries via https://studyandlearn.guide.

Interior design by Kathleen Dyson

Library of Congress Cataloging-in-Publication Data has been applied for.

ISBN: 978-1-7369182-5-8 (paperback)
ISBN: 978-1-7369182-4-1 (ebook)

To my parents, Robert Ernest Yancy, Jr. and Delsie Moore Yancy,
for teaching me, my siblings, and countless others
how much fun studying and learning could be!

Contents

Foreword

Dr. Saundra McGuire is a world-renowned expert on teaching and learning with an outstanding track record for helping students find their path to academic success. Her latest book is a must for any parent or student who wants to unlock the mysteries of achieving academic success in high school. *The Parents' Guide to Studying and Learning* is a practical guide to what it takes to achieve success in *all* aspects of classroom preparation and how parents and students can work together to make sure the correct steps are taken in the journey to achievement. This dynamic and practical book is divided into three areas of interest: learning and studying, emotions and motivation, and the nuts and bolts of putting it all together. Each section is easy to read and full of practical advice and strategies for academic success.

One of the most valued sections of the book is the one in which Dr McGuire discusses the scary prospect of "dealing with failure." Failure is something we all fear in our learning efforts, but the reality is that we learn the most when we recover from failure. Anyone who has taken a test and not done as well as they wished understands that going over the wrong answers and correcting the mistake is one of the most vital learning strategies available to the learner. Dr McGuire outlines her method of how to achieve ultimate success from any academic failure. Three Appendices in the book offer practical advice on Test Prep, Study Tools, and How to Find a Tutor.

Having worked in college admissions for more than 40 years I have interacted with thousands of students and their parents. I have watched as students entered college and struggled for success due to poor study skills or uncertainty of their academic talents. The high schools of America vary in how they prepare students for college. Even bright students who sailed through their high school programs sometimes come up short when they have to tackle college-level classes given poor preparation on how to study, take notes, or thrive in class. It is important to note that college students can get into an early slump and it can take many semesters to turn around their academic profile. If parents and students had early access to Dr McGuire's years of understanding as to how students learn, through *The Parents' Guide to Studying and Learning*, they would have a clear understanding of what it takes to be a good student. Once they achieve this success they will never be satisfied with less.

The Parents' Guide to Studying and Learning is a must read for anyone eager to do better in their academic journey.

—James S. McCoy, PhD
*Vice President for Enrollment Management
at Salem College, Winston Salem, NC*

Introduction: The Power of Learning Strategies

You Can Get Your Child Ready for Success

I wrote this book so that you can get your child ready to be more successful in school, and I want to tell you right off the bat that I know you can do this. Whether you breezed through school or never quite understood why math has to include letters of the alphabet, I'm going to take you on a journey full of "aha" moments that will equip you to transform your child's experience of learning.

The key term is *learning strategies*. A learning strategy is just a simple change to a student's study habits or a shift in attitude that makes it possible for that student to learn more deeply and securely, with much less frustration, despair, or self-punishment. I'm going to show you how to deliver powerful learning strategies to your child that will forever change the way they think about themselves and their learning abilities.

What you need to know up front is that it doesn't matter whether anyone ever taught *you* learning strategies or what level of education you reached. You can successfully teach your child how to learn.

I am here to take you step by step through the method I, and countless other educators, have used to transform students' performance at school and to make learning fun for them.

You Don't Need to Be an Expert

People often mistakenly believe that they must have expertise in a particular subject area in order to help someone *learn* that subject successfully. Here's why that isn't true:

Let's say a teacher asks a student to go into an office to get a book. They tell the student, "It's called *21st Century Teaching*, and it's on the second shelf on the bookcase to your left." The teacher expects the student to be in and out in five seconds, but instead they stay in the office for a long while. When the student does finally emerge, their hands are empty. The teacher says, "Didn't you see the book?"

"Well, it was dark in there."

"You didn't turn on the light?"

"What light?"

"There's a light switch on the wall to the right, just as you walk in. Just flip it up."

"Ohhhh. I didn't know that."

The student goes back in the office and successfully returns with the book a few seconds later. From that point on, the student knows that every dark room they walk into likely has a light switch, and if they turn it on, they can find whatever they need in that room.

Learning strategies are like those light switches. They help students independently find whatever they need in order to gain mastery of what they're learning at school. You don't have to know the subject area. You just have to teach your child how to turn on the light. And I'm going to show you exactly how to do that.

A Brief Word About Language: Parents and Children

Throughout the book, I use the terms "parent" and "child" to describe the person delivering the learning strategies and the person receiving them, respectively. But, of course, any adult is capable of delivering these strategies to any child, whether they are related or not.

I also use the pronoun *they* in its singular form throughout the book because it is the most practical and inclusive approach.

The Power of Learning Strategies—Overnight Success

Let me share with you two emails I recently received, the first from a ninth grader and the second from the parent of a tenth grader. Both students literally saw overnight success. Most information that could be used to identify them has been removed or changed, but I assure you they are real, flesh-and-blood people.

From the student who went to a workshop for students that I presented at her school in Virginia:

Hello,

I am Jennie K_____! I attended your presentation at the _____ School. I would like to tell you that the day you came I got a 79.2 on my physics test. The test is two parts, so that night I went home and studied using your strategies. Today I took the second part and got a 90.

Thanks,

Jennie K_____

9th grade

From the parent of a 10th grader who took part in one of my virtual workshops in Maryland:

During your presentation, I disconnected my headset in order for my son to hear your suggestions on effective reading strategies. My son, David, currently attends _____ HS. Three weeks ago, my son received a 72 on his test for Honors Biology.

Yesterday, I told him to follow your strategy on his next test, which was scheduled for today. David received an 86 on his test today!!! He was so relieved and grateful for the advice. Thank you so much!!

Mandrell B_____

I followed up with Mandrell,[1] who told me that David was still doing very well in honors biology. And don't worry if your child struggles with English, history, or languages instead of math or science. These strategies are effective no matter the subject. They may not work overnight for every student but based on my 50-year experience as an educator, I believe almost any student who consistently uses them will see improvements in their grades. Moreover, if your child is in the small percentage of students who still struggle after faithfully using the strategies, I will tell you in chapter 8 exactly what else to try.

Who Counts as Smart?

For the first three decades of my teaching career, I believed that some students were smart and some weren't so smart. Then, in 1999, I learned something that transformed my thinking. Now I know it's absolutely not true that students are either smart or not smart. Rather, students either have learning strategies that work for them or they don't. I believe that the overwhelming majority of students who aren't doing well in school simply have not found the learning strategies that are right for them. And I want every parent to know that just because your kid may not be doing well in school, *that does not mean your child is not smart*. It just means they haven't yet discovered the strategies they need.

Oh, and the thing that transformed my outlook in 1999? It's called metacognition, and you'll learn all about it in chapter 3.

The Beginning of My Journey Toward Letting Go of the Smart Label

At this point, I want to pull back the curtain and tell you how I went from believing that intelligence is a gift you're born with to believing that it can be discovered, unlocked, and magnified by learning strategies. First off, you should know that both of my daughters did very well in school. So, until about 30 years ago, I had always thought of my kids as *smart kids*. Listening to friends describe the challenges they went through with their children, I even felt like I dodged a bullet because I was lucky enough to have been blessed with *smart kids*.

Yet when I began to understand how powerful effective learning strategies could be, I realized that each of my kids was pretty much like any other kid. It just so happened that their parents and teachers had *taught* them how to be smart. It dawned on me that all of the things my husband and I had done for our daughters had powerfully prepared them to be successful in school. For example, I read to both my girls in the womb because I had read research explaining that, at a certain stage of development, fetuses pick up sounds. So, if they get used to the rising and falling sounds of a language, they have a head start learning that language once they are born. When I used to read to them as little children, I often asked them what they thought might happen next in a story or what kind of stories they might like to write themselves. On top of that, both my husband and I routinely fell into our educators' habits and often answered our girls' questions with more questions, encouraging them to think actively and work things out for themselves. My husband, a professor of physics, often played number games with them and taught them basic programming skills so that they could write their own simple computer games instead of just playing video games you could buy from the store. Instinctively with our actions, we taught our children that information and ideas aren't just things you *consume*, they're things you can analyze, transform, and produce yourself.

But I didn't really realize I was teaching them those lessons until later in my career as an educator, when I met struggling students who were able to transform their academic performance so completely that no one could deny how smart they were. So I had to ask myself: Are my kids *smart*, or were they just *taught how to learn* from a very early age by two experienced educators?

Digging even deeper, I realized that during those times when my kids *weren't* making great grades, my husband and I never assumed that their performance reflected their abilities, partly because we had already labeled them as *smart*! Whenever our girls had trouble in school, we sat down and talked with them in order to get to the bottom of *why* they were not performing as well as we thought they could. We were motivated to ask those questions because we had put them in the category of *smart*, *good students*, and when they weren't doing well, their grades didn't match that labeling. But what if they had become smarter, better students *because* we had always asked those questions when they were having trouble? What came first, the chicken or the egg?

Up to that point, I had always seen my own children's performance in school as evidence that some students were smart and others weren't, but then I realized that my daughters' experiences had actually been trying to tell me the *opposite* story! *Teach a child how to learn, and they can reach their potential.* Today, I firmly believe that anyone at any time—including your child, no matter what grade they are in—can be taught how to learn and eventually reach their goals in school and in life. And you don't have to be a professor to successfully teach your children these learning strategies.

How I Saw the Light and Discovered the Power of Learning Strategies

Now I want to share with you my *professional* journey in discovering the difference that learning strategies can make. My academic training is in how to teach chemistry. From the time I had to start teaching, in graduate school, I discovered that I was pretty decent at it. Students seemed to get what I was trying to explain to them. I even won awards.

But what I didn't understand at that point is that *learning always trumps teaching*. In other words, the most skillful, wonderful teacher cannot reach a student who has poor learning skills. But a skilled learner? *A skilled learner can survive any kind of teaching.* Before

I realized that crucial point, I concentrated on being able to relay information to students in as many ways as I needed to until they understood what I was trying to teach them. But I was clueless about teaching students *how to learn*. To use a popular analogy, I could catch a lot of fish and give them to my students, but I couldn't yet teach them how to fish. Yet I was fortunate enough that my expert fishing abilities took me to Cornell University, where my husband had accepted a position as a professor. I was offered a job as assistant director of the student learning center, a position that came with a joint teaching position in the chemistry department. My daily duties were mostly teaching chemistry to first- and second-year students and helping them master the subject. It was the perfect fit, and eventually I became director of the center.

At the learning center, I met a wonderful educator named Helene Selco, whose title was *learning strategist*. I didn't really know what she did with students, but I also figured that I didn't need to know. After all, I was there to teach chemistry, not learning strategies. So every time my approach wasn't working for a student, I would just send them to Dr. Selco for assistance. Yet at the same time, I started finding my own way toward teaching people how to fish for themselves. As I worked with student after student, I began to see patterns. Within the first year, I had figured out why many students weren't doing well, and I made some suggestions that worked for them. It was the first time I saw how students could go from failing one week to making As and Bs the next week. But although I was helping students and stumbling onto some of the learning strategies, I didn't have my big aha moment until my next job.

After 10 years of brutal winters at Cornell, my husband was asked to head the physics department at the college we both graduated from, Southern University in Baton Rouge, Louisiana. Since we grew up in Louisiana, we decided it was time to return home. I looked into my options, and sure enough, the learning center director at LSU was leaving. I applied, interviewed, and happily accepted an offer. I expected to do exactly what I had done at Cornell, but there was a catch! The person who taught learning strategies was on maternity leave, so I would be expected to do what *she* did with students. That stroke of fate changed the direction of my entire life.

The learning strategies people at LSU—particularly a brilliant woman named Sarah Baird—opened my eyes. All of a sudden I had an explanation for so many of the things I had observed up to that point in my teaching career. I started getting powerful tools for teaching students how to net huge harvests of fish. But I'll level with you. At first, when I learned what Sarah was teaching, I thought her strategies were too simple and straightforward to be of real use to students. It wasn't until I began to see students who started out making Ds and Fs come back into my office a few weeks later with As and Bs that I understood how wrong I had been. Sure, I had seen that kind of turnaround occasionally at Cornell, but now I was seeing it *much* more often. I remember thinking to myself, "Oh this stuff actually works. I'd better pay closer attention to what's going on here."

I read everything I could get my hands on and began exploring the very best way to transform students' lives with learning strategies. Within a couple of years, the chemistry department invited me to become a professor, and I started helping other science instructors use learning strategies to help their students succeed. Eventually, I began to help instructors who taught all kinds of subjects, including history, English, and physical education. During that time, I became convinced that learning strategies can help *any* student learn *anything* at *any* level. In fact, for the past 20 years, I've been on a mission to spread learning strategies as far and wide as possible. I want you to have this book so that *your* child can experience the power of learning strategies. And it's okay if you're skeptical, or if your child is skeptical, because I was too! By the time you finish the book, I hope you'll be persuaded.

Other Parents' Experiences Also Strengthened My Convictions about the Power of Learning Strategies

As I was undergoing my change of heart at LSU, one other source of information helped convince me of how powerful learning strategies could be: the experiences of other parents. Time and again, I would hear stories about students who, at one time, had not been doing well. But when their parents sat down and went through their homework with them, helping them to slow down and actively think about what they were trying to learn, their performance turned around. My methods are more detailed than that—and those details are the key to their effectiveness—but at their root, they are based on a very simple idea.

Yes, people have done very academic, complex research in order to give us confidence that learning strategies work. But I don't want you to lose sight of the fact that at the end of the day, it's all about slowing down and taking the time to engage with what we want to learn in the ways that make the most sense for us as individuals. So I predict that everything in this book, when you look at it in hindsight, will seem simple and obvious to you. That's why many students are able to stumble upon these strategies without needing to be taught them. It's how my husband and I were able to instinctively give so many of them to our own children.

You Can Do It

Your experience of working through this book, with the companion website, has been designed to address and alleviate any fears or resistance you or your child may be feeling. A lot of care has gone into creating a system so that you can *confidently* do what I and countless other learning-strategy experts have done for students of every kind. All of the resources provided have been carefully crafted with your experience in mind at every turn. I want you to feel as supported as possible in giving your child everything they may need to excel.

Who Is This Book For?

This book is definitely for you if you can relate to one or more of the following statements:

- My child is not doing well in school, and I don't know how to help them.

- I have a sense that my child could be doing better in school.

- My child is doing well in school, but I want them to get more out of their learning.

- I homeschool but worry about whether my child is learning everything they should.

- I was forced to homeschool during the pandemic and worry my child is behind.

- My child got behind while doing virtual lessons during the pandemic and I want to help them catch up.

- My child has ADHD, dyslexia, another learning-disability diagnosis, or is otherwise neurodiverse, and I don't want that to diminish their learning or ruin their experience at school.

- My child may be headed for technical or vocational school, conservatory, or a professional career straight out of high school, but I want them to know they are still as academically capable as kids who go the traditional college route.

- I want my child to be optimally prepared for their college experience.

- I want my child to experience more joy and pleasure in learning.

I Promise that by the Time You Finish Reading This Book You Will:

- Understand why your child may not be doing as well as they could in school.

- Know exactly how to share transformative learning strategies with your child.

- Know why something called *metacognition* is such a game changer for students.

- Know how to support your child's thinking and learning so that it is both skillful and joyful.

- Be prepared to see your child's grades rise.

A Warm Welcome

At this point, please head over to the website, www.studyandlearn.guide, and watch the introduction video I've recorded for you.

CHAPTER 1

How My Method Works and How to Use This Book

Why My Method Is a Game Changer

All of the learning strategies in this book are based on cognitive science principles shown through research to be valid. But if all of these strategies are proven and have already been around for a while, what's so special about my framework? Why has it been a game changer for so many students and educators?

Let me give you a little background: Human beings are built to resist change (even though we are also built to seek out new experiences). We have a little scorekeeper in our heads that keeps track of what makes us feel better and what makes us feel worse. And it steers us toward what makes us feel better in the short term. That's why, despite the fact that most people know *what* to do in order to get healthy, most people also find it very difficult to consistently get more exercise, drink more water, and get enough sleep.

My method for transforming student performance puts that scorekeeper front and center. It makes students aware of all of the good, fun, enjoyable things that will happen if they change their behavior. It fires up students' motivation and also uses the power of their emotions to support their learning. That's why it's a game changer—it packages strategies for deeper learning *with* strategies for behavioral change into one powerful system that is easy to introduce.

My method also addresses time-management struggles. In addition to helping students with full and busy lives plan enough study time, my system also helps to make sure they stick with their new habits in the long term. In other words, my method acknowledges students' full humanity instead of treating them like compliant learning robots.

Because I developed this method over a number of years, through trial and error, and have used it for more than two decades now, I have learned to distinguish the parts that are essential and mandatory from the parts that can be tailored to individual situations. Most everything in the method is deceptively simple, so I am asking you to trust that if you go through it step by step according to my recommendations, you will be most likely to see results. If you do some steps out of order, or skip them altogether, the program may not be as effective as it could be. ***Chapter 12 provides you with an easy-to-follow road map for how to present the strategies, handouts, and worksheets to your child.*** Choose the pacing that works best for your schedule, your child's schedule, and your child's needs.

Enjoying Success Is Addictive

I created this image to show how teaching people *how* to learn can lead to a snowball effect that totally transforms their futures. I call it the cycle of motivation. Remember that scorekeeper in our heads? When better grades make a student feel good, then the scorekeeper reminds them that they want to repeat that experience. That gives them the motivation to continue to do the work of deep, durable learning, which will in turn allow them to keep their grades up.

Increased motivation → Increased learning → Increased success → Positive emotions →

Part of the reason my method is so finely tuned is that I know a lot is riding on how a student responds to the strategies. If I can get a student to change their study habits within 48 hours of meeting me, those changes might trigger a domino effect of experiences and decisions that end up giving the student a career and life that they love. But the more time that passes after our meeting, the less likely it is that the student will put into practice the changes I've suggested. That's why the student's first encounter with the strategies is so important to me. I can't tell you the number of times I've had a version of the following conversation:

> Student: "Oh, I wish I had come to see you at the beginning of the year."
>
> Me: "Would you mind telling me why you didn't?"
>
> Student: "Well, I didn't know *this* is what you were going to tell me. I thought you were just going to say stuff that I'd heard a million times before that I was already trying to do. I thought it was going to just make me feel worse and more like a failure."

You can see that when the learning strategies are presented effectively, then students already start to understand—*while* they're hearing about them—how the strategies are different from the things they've been told to do in the past, and why they have the power to make a real difference in their lives. If I can convince a student to do something they've never done before by using these learning strategies, then that student will have a personal experience of discovering that the strategies do, in fact, work. Then the cycle of motivation can take over.

How to Use This Book

I am so excited to share this information with you, and I want so much for your child to experience success, that I have included lots of handouts, activities, worksheets, planning tools, and scripts for you and your child to use. But I also know that you have limited time, and I want this process to go smoothly for you. So I'm going to take the next several sections to explain exactly how this book is designed and how you can use it in a way that works best for you and your family.

In Some Parts of This Book I Talk to You; in Other Parts, I Talk to Your Child; and in Others, You Talk to Your Child

The ideas in this book really have two intended recipients: both you and your child. So, sometimes I talk directly to you; sometimes I guide you in how to deliver information to your child; and in some places I talk directly to your child. For example, although this book is addressed to you, most of the handouts are addressed to your child.

To sum it up, sometimes the flow of information goes like this:

ME ➔ YOU

sometimes it goes like this:

ME ➔ YOU ➔ YOUR CHILD

and sometimes it goes like this:

ME ➔ YOUR CHILD.

You could think of this book like the teacher's edition of a textbook, although I hope reading it is much more enjoyable. Because it's structured this way, you should read the *whole* book before you start sharing the ideas with your child. Once you've got the lay of the land, you'll be better equipped to lead your child through it.

Your Road Map

Step 1: Read this book from front to back.

Step 2: From a range of options laid out in chapter 12, choose how you'd like to lead your child through the Core Content outlined in that chapter.

Step 3: Print out the relevant handouts and worksheets for your child or arrange for them to appear on their tablet or laptop.

Step 4: Deliver these strategies to your child in as little as three days or over a longer period of time that works best for your family.

Why Handouts?

I've included more than 50 handouts—many of them optional—so that your child can *actively* learn the information in this book. Some of the handouts are worksheets that they get to fill out or do activities with. The idea is to give them an engaging, interactive experience similar to what would happen if they attended one of my workshops. The worksheets should not feel like homework or busy work. So, if you know your child struggles with sitting down to focus, just talk through the worksheets with them. On the other hand, if you know your child is quiet and thoughtful and likes to be left alone, then give them a few minutes to work through the worksheets on their own before they share their answers with you. I recommend in many places for your child to read handouts aloud, but if you know your child hates that, then reading quietly to themselves is totally fine. None of this is supposed to be difficult, challenging, or torturous for your kid. The opposite, in fact! Anyone who knows me will tell you that I'm a big believer in fun as a source of energy and motivation.

The other purpose of the handouts is to give your child something concrete to hold onto and refer to long after your conversations with them are over. By the time you are done with them, they will have their own booklet of material, including several pages of planning and study tools. This booklet could be as short as 20 pages or as long as 60 pages, depending on what your child wants and needs.

In chapter 7 I ask you to think through several of the worksheets from your own perspective, and in chapter 8, there's one worksheet for you as a parent to fill out. There are also handouts and worksheets for parents in chapter 12 to help you map out your conversations with your child.

How to Use the Scripts (There's Nothing You Need to Memorize!)

In order to ensure that you have the best shot at confidently delivering these learning strategies to your child, I have given you scripts to use in the early chapters where the information is a little more specialized. For people who might dislike the idea of being tied to the exact words in my scripts, I have provided a list of points at the end of each script that summarizes the information you need to deliver to your child. These lists are called *script summaries*. So people who feel more comfortable with the idea of being able to read exactly what their child needs to hear should use the scripts, while people who like to flow more freely can use the script summaries. Some people may mix the approaches and stick to the script in some places but work from the summaries in others.

The idea for both groups of people is that during your initial read through of the book, you'll familiarize yourself with the information, so that when you read the script to your child or deliver the information using the summaries, you can be both accurate *and* engaging. Those parents using scripts should do their best to deliver the information with warmth and joy, while those parents using summaries should do the same, while making sure they are being accurate.

During the later chapters that deal with emotion and motivation, there are no scripts because so much of how you choose to deliver the content depends on your child's individual personality. Instead, I talk directly to you during those chapters and give you handouts and worksheets you can use to present the ideas to your child. So instead of scripts or script summaries, chapters 8–11 give you summary lists of all the handouts—called handout roundups—with details about how to use each one. You can think of the handout roundups in chapters 8–11 as comparable to the script summaries in chapters 3–7. In chapter 12, I give you a concrete framework for delivering the strategies and lay out exactly which resources to use at what time. But the pacing with which you deliver these resources is up to you, according to the needs of your child and your family.

A Map of the Journey

Now that we've established the materials that you'll be using, let's go through exactly what this book covers.

Chapter 2 is just me talking to you. I give you a preview of the different types of material in the book, and we also talk about what learning is and how it may or may not be connected to grades. Then I give you some ideas about why your child probably doesn't know how to learn yet. (Spoiler alert: it's no one's fault.) The rest of the book unfolds as follows:

- Chapters 3–6 cover the ins and outs of learning and studying, including 10 metacognitive learning strategies to boost your child's performance in school.

- Chapters 7–9 deal with emotions and motivation—how to get your child to consistently *use* the learning strategies.

- Chapters 10–12 are about the nuts and bolts of making it happen and getting it done—when, where, and how.

At the back of the book, I've included bonus material for exam preparation, a deep dive into different study tools, and a step-by-step guide to hiring a tutor. There's also a page of recommended resources and some references for further reading.

The Website—Where the Handouts Are Located

I mentioned earlier that sometimes the information flows ME ➜ YOU, and sometimes it flows ME ➜ YOUR CHILD. This book is the container for the information that I want to flow from me to you. After all, it's called *The Parents' Guide to Studying and Learning*. But all of the information that is directed toward your child is in a different place, on this book's companion online platform, a website (www.studyandlearn.guide) that houses all of this book's supplements: the handouts, worksheets, and guides.

However, some of the resources for your child contain crucial information that you also need to know. Whenever that's the case, I have reproduced those resources here in this book so that you have easy access to them. Just before the end of each chapter, there's a breakdown of that chapter's handouts and where you can find them—on the web, in the book, or both.

This system gives you the best of both worlds. You have all the information you need, but your reading isn't bogged down by having to page through endless handouts.

Using the Website as You Read

There is another advantage to having all of the supplements on the website. Having the material for you and the material for your child in two different places is preparing you to step into a teaching role. Every time you visit the website to look at handouts for your child, you are there as someone in a teaching role, as someone who intends to deliver information and an experience to your child. While you are reading the book, however, you are in the role of learner. Having two separate contexts enables you to flow between these two roles so that they are distinct but connected.

I encourage you in several places to visit the website while you are reading, in order to gradually get comfortable with the resources you will eventually deliver to your child. That small pause between looking up from the book and visiting the website to discover what your child will encounter there is intended to be a refreshing moment for you, a way of deepening your learning by giving you a second to pause and breathe. If for some reason you prefer not to visit the website while you are reading, your experience as a learner will not suffer. Everything you need to understand this book is within its pages. But I think that the sooner you can get comfortable using the website, the more you will find it helpful for stepping into the role of teacher with ease and being able to confidently deliver the information to your child.

I know you are likely busy, overscheduled, and overworked, and so this experience has been designed to be as efficient and resistance-free as possible. The website has been thoughtfully created as a tool to prepare you—with as much ease and enjoyment as possible—to work effectively with your child.

Linking Up with Other Parents to Go Through This Process Together

It's great if you want to go through this process on your own, just you and your child. But if you prefer a feeling of fellowship, you might suggest to another parent, or a group of parents, that you read this book together. When I was getting feedback about the book I wrote for college teachers, I was surprised to learn that many of them had found it helpful to read the book in a group with other teachers, or even just in pairs. So, if you're part of a regular book club, you could think about suggesting this as your next pick. Or you could simply contact another parent and see if they're interested in informal get togethers.

A Welcoming Note to Parents of Neurodiverse Students as well as Students with Alternate Career Paths

Sometimes school can feel like a hostile place for kids who correctly sense that they are different from most people. Whether your child feels different because they are neuroatypical and have a diagnosis like ADHD,* or because they are destined for a different future than most of their peers, my sincere hope is that the ideas in this book empower them to confidently embrace their uniqueness as a superpower. At their core, my learning strategies are based on knowing what's best for us as individual learners at any given moment. I hope they will be particularly useful for unconventional learners. The Recommended Resources section includes books and websites relevant to this group of students. Let me make it clear, though, that I believe that almost every student *can* succeed in college. The question is just whether that's the best choice for them given their gifts, goals, and personality.

A Welcoming Note to Homeschooling Parents

Whether you've been temporarily drafted into the homeschooling ranks or you're in it for the long haul, I had you in mind while constructing this book. One of the advantages of homeschooling is that children get used to learning without the structure of school and large classes. The content of this book fits well with the homeschool model because it is about *independent learning*. In other words, we have students who are being asked to learn more independently, at home instead of at school, and so those students are primed to absorb the tools of independent learning. In turn, those tools provide a particular benefit to those students *because* they are being asked to learn more independently. My hope is that homeschooling parents find this book especially useful. Because you have flexibility in creating your lesson plans, you may even want to use the resources here to teach an entire unit about learning.

What If I Don't Have a Good Relationship with My Child?

Even if you have a difficult relationship with your child and feel like they do the opposite of whatever you say, you can still make sure they are introduced to these learning strategies. After you finish this book, either ask an adult your child listens to or hire a tutor to read the book and deliver its contents. But even if that's your plan, please do keep reading. If someone other than you ends up communicating this information to your child, it will still be very useful for you to know what they are learning so that you can gently reinforce the concepts whenever you have an opportunity. Appendix C guides you through the process of finding a tutor, either to deliver learning strategies or for specific subjects.

---

* The information in this book is not intended to be a substitute for professional medical advice and should not be relied on as such. Psychologists, psychiatrists, or other qualified mental health professionals should be involved in the educational planning of all neurodiverse students. I have included recommended resources pointing parents to resources they may find useful. The information in this book is presented from the perspective that mental health conditions that make learning challenging can sometimes respond to simple strategies.

If your child is highly motivated and a self-starter, it may also work to simply give them this book to read themselves. For more advanced students, you could give them the book that this one is based on: *Teach Yourself How to Learn.*

Optional Reading

Teach Yourself How to Learn is a book I wrote primarily for students in college, but it has also been used by many high school students. Reading this more in-depth treatment of the concepts and strategies outlined here in *The Parent's Guide* will make you even better prepared to introduce them to your child. And the more effective you are at delivering the strategies, the likelier they are to boost your child's academic performance. You will also get a glimpse of the optimal preparation that students need in order to do well in college. Additionally, if you are interested in references pointing to the research underpinning my recommendations, you'll find them in *Teach Yourself How to Learn.*

Motivation, Learning, and Grades: How They're Connected

Learning and How We Feel About Learning Are Two Sides of the Same Coin

In the previous chapter, I said that my system combines evidence-based learning strategies with methods for shifting a student's frame of mind in order to inspire effective behavioral changes. Students have their eyes opened to how it's *possible* for them succeed, and then they're motivated to work harder. As a result of their hard work, they learn more and do better in school.

Because it's a system with a two-pronged approach, this book is divided into roughly two halves.

- Chapters 3–6 lay out everything you need to know about learning and studying—how to think about it, how to do it, and various strategies and tools your child can use. I call this the *Learning* half of the book.

- Chapters 7–11 deal with all of the less concrete stuff that affects your child's learning—emotions, mindset, and motivation—as well as the nuts and bolts of planning and time management. I call this the *Mindset, Motivation, and Planning* half of the book.

This chapter will give you a taste of the *Learning* half and then a taste of the *Mindset, Motivation, and Planning* half so that you can begin to imagine how the two types of material fit together. Think of it like this: The basics of studying and learning are like the bricks of a house. But mindset and motivation are like the mortar, the stuff that glues the bricks together. So if you want your child to establish good learning habits that last a lifetime, you'll want to give equal consideration to the bricks *and* the mortar. If you just stick to the *Learning* part because it seems like "the important stuff," you might get stuck with a bunch of well-formed bricks laying around instead of a nice, sturdy building that will stand the test of time.

A Powerful Learning Strategy: Using Homework to Test Depth of Understanding

Of the 10 learning strategies I present in Chapter 6, this strategy is one of the most powerful. If you were anything like me when I was in school, you did your homework by reading a problem or question and then looking for an example in your notes or in your textbook to follow along with, step by step. It makes sense, right? When we want to do something, we look for a step-by-step guide.

But although it's a logical thing to do, this is the wrong way to go about doing homework if our goal is to securely, deeply *learn* something. Instead, students should prepare for doing assigned homework by studying all of their reading assignments and notes—chapters 3–6 detail exactly how to go about doing that—and then *put it all away*. Next, they should take out their homework assignment and try to do it without looking at any notes, guides, or other assistance. Only if they get stuck should they take a peek at their notes, but only at the specific section that might help them with the part of the problem or question that they're working on right then. After that, they should continue—without assistance—until the next time they get stuck and take another brief look at their notes, or until they finish the problem or question. In chapter 6, I explain this strategy in greater detail. But I hope you can already imagine how doing homework this way can transform a student's grades. When students use this strategy, they are training their brains to do exactly what it must do on a quiz or a test—solve problems independently and without help, using only the information and concepts that the student can recall and retrieve from memory.

This one strategy is responsible for so many of the overnight turnarounds I've seen in my students. One of the most impressive was pulled off by a fellow named Adam. He had scored 65%, 61%, and 61% on his first three chemistry exams. But after meeting with me two days before the final exam and using this homework strategy alongside a few others I give in chapter 6, Adam scored 107% on his final exam! The grader was actually convinced that he had cheated, but I explained that Adam had actually had a lot of information in his head a few days before the test. He just hadn't been able to convert that knowledge into deeper *learning* or good grades.

Adam's Shift in Mindset Was Also Crucial for His Success

Our *mindset*, as defined by Stanford psychologist Carol S. Dweck, determines whether we *believe* we can improve our performance in a particular area. Do we believe that how smart we are is something that's mostly fixed, like our height, or do we believe that *we can get smarter through effort*? You can imagine that when we believe intelligence is fixed, we end up deciding that there are lots of things we aren't capable of. But when we believe our intelligence can grow, we become willing to put in the work to *make* it grow. Put another way, it's important to believe we can succeed because if we think we *can't* do something, we usually don't try very hard! That's why our mindset is such a big deal. Your child must be convinced that their *future behavior* matters much more than what they have done in the past. This is especially true if they have a history of struggling with schoolwork. We want to shift their focus from *how smart others think they are* to *the actions they take*.

One of the most important things that happened during my session with Adam is that—when he saw how the strategies I was sharing with him were different from what he'd been doing before—he started to understand that 65%, 61%, and 61% were only reflections of his past *behavior* and had nothing to do with *who he was and what he was capable of*. He began to understand that he held the power to change his behavior, deepen his learning, and raise his grades.

What About Your Mindset?

I think you're starting to see how learning strategies and students' attitudes are intertwined. As soon as students receive concrete, commonsense learning strategies, a lightbulb goes on and they see: *Oh, I got those grades in the past because I wasn't doing the right stuff. If I start doing the right stuff, I'll get different results.* Then, once I tell them about mindset explicitly, their belief that they can change becomes even stronger.

One of my intentions in publishing this book is to change *your* mindset on two levels. First, I want you to understand that your child's grades may not have anything to do with their potential. I want you to believe that any one of us, including your child, can get smarter with effort. Second, I want you to believe that even if you've unsuccessfully tried to help your child improve their learning in the past, that doesn't necessarily mean anything about your future with them. This book is going to give you concrete, commonsense things to do to help your child, so that you can get different results than you've gotten in the past.

You, in the Roles of Learner and Teacher

You'll be absorbing the material in this book in order to pass it on to your child. So, in addition to having me with you every step of the way, I've also provided a few handouts and worksheets for you, to help strengthen your understanding. On top of that, I encourage you to work through the worksheets in chapter 7 before your child does so that you can more closely examine your own beliefs about intelligence and academic ability. Letting go of any harmful beliefs about these things, and adopting helpful ones, can have a profound impact on both you and your child. The more you believe in yourself as a learner, the more you'll be able to teach your child to believe in themselves.

Now that we've looked at the connections between learning and our attitude about it, let's take a deeper look at the relationship between *grades* and learning. Adam's example has already made clear that there is not always a straightforward connection between the two.

The Relationship Between Grades and Learning: What Is Learning?

There are many ways to define *learning*, some more complicated than others. Right now, I want to connect with your gut feeling of what it means to learn. When we have really learned something, we often have a deep knowing about it in our bones. We have a feeling of mastery, a sense of confidence like, "Oh yeah, I know how to do that." What often leads to that kind of deep learning is an eager pursuit of our own genuine curiosity. And we can activate that kind of curiosity and learning even for things that may not interest us when we first encounter them. I'm not suggesting that we can get interested in *anything*—we all have limits and preferences—but the range of things we can become curious about and learn is so much bigger than the range of things we're interested in right off the bat. Most of the time, we just need to understand how the things we're not interested in *are related to* the things that we do care about. When we're curious and interested, learning is fun. And my mission is for everyone, especially children and teens, to understand how enjoyable and rewarding learning can be.

The Relationship Between Grades and Learning: What Are Grades?

Grades reflect the habits and behaviors that a particular student engaged in before they completed the quiz, test, homework, or other assessment that was graded. But often, grades are interpreted as a reflection of a student's intelligence or potential. In so many cases, nothing could be further from the truth. Grades can tell us what a student *has* been doing. They cannot tell us what a student is *capable* of doing.

Many people interpret grades as a reflection of your child's potential. So, if your goal is to persuade people to see your child in a different light, you may need to challenge some conventional wisdom. But that's okay. You can choose to see people who may be underestimating your child not as adversaries who need to be defeated but instead as fallible human beings who are just drawing conclusions based on their experience up to that point in their lives. You can think to yourself how delighted they will be to be proven wrong and to see your child soar. You can smile to yourself as you imagine how their experience with you and your child will transform the way they treat students in the future. Remember, I also used to see grades as a reflection of a student's ability and potential. And now look at me, passionately traveling the country to spread the message that all students can excel, *if* we teach them how.

Do Good Grades Always Indicate High-Quality Learning?

So now we know that poor grades don't always reflect a student's potential to learn. But do good grades always reflect deep learning? Let me tell you a story. When my younger daughter was in college, she got As in chemistry. One of her friends struggled to get average grades. One day, they were having a conversation, and my daughter realized that her friend knew a lot more about chemistry than she did and understood many concepts much more deeply than she did. In that moment, my daughter realized that her excellent memory and pattern-recognition skills were compensating for a lack of deep understanding. In an oral exam, her friend would have wiped the floor with her. Sure enough, the next year, my daughter struggled to keep her grades up in a higher-level chemistry class and ultimately decided not to take more difficult, optional chemistry classes, even though they would have been very useful to reach the career goal she had back then, which was to become a biology researcher. She remembers sitting in class thinking that if she had understood the previous year's material as well as her friend, she wouldn't be struggling.

In my daughter's case, good grades were able to conceal a lack of deep learning because she was compensating with a great short-term memory and crackerjack test-taking skills. But sometimes good grades can cover up shallow learning because a student may not be challenged enough. If school is too comfortable for a student and they don't have to work that hard to ace their classes, you can introduce them to the idea that there will be bigger ponds for them to swim in and oceans where deep learning will be required to stay afloat.

Why Doesn't My Child Already Know How to Learn?

Your child has probably never been *taught* how to learn. I am in no way suggesting that teachers are not doing their jobs. They are absolutely doing their jobs under the most difficult of circumstances, and I will go to the mat to defend and support our underappreciated, underpaid teaching corps. It's just that our current educational system—especially with its emphasis on high-stakes testing—does not prioritize giving students strategies for deep, lasting learning.

Another possible answer to this question could be that your child hasn't really *had* to know how to learn in order to get by in school up to this point. (My daughter isn't the only one who can get by on a good memory and pattern-recognition skills!) This can happen either because the expectations set for them have been too low or because the challenges that they've been given could be greater. Or possibly both. Whatever the reason, I see this all the time with incoming first-year college students. They did well in high school with certain study habits, and when those habits don't cut it in college, they freak out and think they're big failures. But the truth is that they didn't get the tools they need in order to excel *in college*. You may also be experiencing this kind of thing if your child is navigating a tough transition between middle and high school, or from a less competitive to a more competitive school.

The thing is, even if you try to get ahead of the game and prepare your child for a big jump in difficulty, sometimes there's not really a way for them to imagine it until it happens to them. In my workshops with teachers, I tell them it's like saying to a student, "You're going to another planet next month, and when you get there, you've got to breathe differently." They might hear the words, but they have no way of interpreting them without the direct experience of the new situation.

Is My Child Lazy? Or Just Being Smart?

One big turning point in my own journey was realizing that students who were slouching in their seats, looking like they had dragged themselves to class after a big party the night before, had no idea that they weren't on track to succeed in my class. Even though they weren't turning in well-executed homework assignments or following what was going on in class, they figured that they could just do what they'd always done in the past—cram the night before and do well enough to pass or even do well. I realized that I could turn my frustration into insight. Instead of thinking, "Aargh, why don't these kids get it together and realize they need to make some effort?!" I started thinking, "Ah, so they're just being logical. They're using what has worked for them in the past and applying it to a new situation." Even if you have a child who has always struggled with their schoolwork, from their perspective, they have still managed to *survive*. So what they're doing is working, by at least one definition, and it's logical for them to continue doing it. I realized that in order for my slacker students to change their behavior, they would have to be convinced that what they were doing *wasn't* working for them, *and* they would need to know what to do in order to get different results.

This transition in my thinking totally transformed how I treated my students. I stopped thinking that struggling students who seemed to me like they couldn't care less were unmotivated or lazy. Once I understood that they were actually behaving sensibly, I could give them respect rather than disdain. And I could recognize that all they needed were some strategies to improve their learning. I hope my experience can give you a more empowering perspective on any aspects of your child's attitude and behavior that you may find frustrating.

All Progress Should Be Enthusiastically Celebrated!

In the introduction to this book, we learned about David, a 10th grader who raised his biology test grades from 72 to 86, and Jennie, a ninth grader who raised her physics test grades from 79 to 90, both of them overnight. I've also told you about Adam, who went from having an F average to getting 107% on his final exam in two days.

Let me say here that although I can tell you dozens and dozens of stories like the ones above, I also realize that they are exceptional. I have shared strategies with thousands of students in my lifetime, and of course not everyone gets results this dramatic. I fully admit I am doing what data scientists call "cherry-picking" in order to get your attention and show you how powerful these strategies can be. But I also have hundreds more stories of less dramatic progress, and I celebrate those just as enthusiastically. When a student brings their B+ up to an A-, their C up to a B, or their F up to a C, I cheer *just as hard* as I do for my failing students who become A students. Those smaller differences can make a huge difference to the range of someone's possibilities or the trajectory of their life.

So whether or not your child experiences an astonishing turnaround or more modest progress by using the learning strategies I'm about to give you, please know that I'm waving my pompoms high for everyone. And I encourage you to do the same.

Thinking About Thinking: Why It's a Game Changer

Metacognition Is Just a Fancy Word for Thinking about Thinking

Metacognition is just *thinking* about thinking. In other words, it's taking a step back from our automatic thinking processes and shining a light on them in order to have more awareness about what we're doing. With that extra awareness, we can improve the ways we think and solve problems. I usually tell my students that **metacognition is like you have a big brain outside of your brain looking at what your brain is doing**. The big brain can see what your brain is doing and make suggestions for how it might do things better.[2]

A researcher named John Flavell coined the term *metacognition* in 1976. Here are four features of his definition that I also explain in my book *Teach Yourself How to Learn*:

Metacognition is:

- The ability to think about your own thinking

- The ability to recognize that you have the power to solve problems

- The ability to plan, supervise, and control your mental processing

- The ability to accurately judge how well you have learned something

Why Metacognition Is Useful

If someone has the ability to step back from their own thinking and *think* about it from an outside perspective, then they can change their thinking in helpful ways. Imagine someone trapped in a maze. Without metacognition, they could be staggering around for days, trying to escape purely through trial and error. But if they're able to watch themselves trying to get out of the maze (bullet 1), then they can plan different strategies and analyze which ones didn't work (bullets 2 and 3). They can *control* their future attempts to get out of the maze instead of being at the mercy of random guessing (bullet 3). If they can *accurately* judge how well they have learned the maze through all their attempts to get out up to that point (bullet 4), then their future attempts are much more likely to be successful. If, on the other hand, they are overconfident about knowing the maze, that cockiness will slow down their escape.

In fact, being able to accurately judge how well we've learned something is one of the biggest benefits of metacognition. We don't feel motivated to go deeper with our learning efforts unless we actually realize that those efforts haven't been adequate. But it's the most human thing in the world to misjudge the depth of our understanding. Have you ever had the experience of thinking that you did well on a test, an essay, or a project, only to get it back with a terrible grade at the top? That has happened to me, both my children, and countless students I know. If it's happened to you, then we share the experience of not having accurately judged how well we have learned something. Metacognition can help us avoid those unpleasant surprises.

When someone is aware of their own thinking processes and can figure out how to solve their own problems, then whenever they come up against an obstacle or a roadblock, they will automatically start looking for solutions instead of waiting for someone else to tell them what to do. In this way, metacognition helps students become independent, confident, and creative learners. When I learned about metacognition, I became a much more skillful educator partly because I got so much better at solving my *own* problems!

Metacognition is such a game changer because, when a student knows how to learn, they can learn in a much broader range of situations. They can even thrive in spite of a style of teaching that might not be a good fit for them. That's why I like to prioritize skillful learning over skillful teaching, although both are important. You can have the best teachers in the world, but if students don't know how to learn, results will be limited. On the other hand, a classroom of expert learners will flourish even with, say, a physics teacher who has been ambushed at the last minute and forced to bluff their way through teaching chemistry because of budget cuts.

Showing You How Metacognition Works: An Activity for You

You're going take your child through this exercise later, but first you'll do it yourself. You have two options: do the exercise by following the instructions on the following pages or access a short video on www.studyandlearn.guide and do it that way. **You can skip the next five pages if you want to do the activity with the video.**

Before you turn the page to start, you will need three things:

- A cellphone or timer you can set for 45 seconds

- A sheet of paper to cover page 19 once you turn the page to page 18

- A pen or pencil

OK, have you got your timer, sheet of paper, and a pen or pencil? Great. Now set your timer for 45 seconds. You're going to do these three things in quick succession once you start your timer:

1. Turn to page 18

2. Cover page 19 with your sheet of paper

3. Count all of the vowels in the words in the box on page 18

Turn the page to begin the exercise.

Count the Vowels

Dollar bill	Cat lives
Dice	Bowling pins
Tricycle	Football team
Four-leaf clover	Dozen eggs
Hand	Unlucky Friday
Six-pack	Valentine's Day
Seven-Up	Quarter hour
Octopus	

When your timer goes off after 45 seconds, move your sheet of paper to cover up *this* page, and read the instructions on the next page.

Now list as many of the words from the box on the previous page as you can remember. Keep your eyes fixed on this page. No cheating!

_____   _____

_____   _____

_____   _____

_____   _____

_____   _____

_____   _____

_____   _____

After you have written down as many of the words as you can, put the number of items you could remember here: _____

Now find your score on this table and write it here: _____

Items remembered	Score
1	7%
2	13%
3	20%
4	27%
5	33%
6	40%
7	47%
8	53%
9	60%
10	67%
11	73%
12	80%
13	87%
14	93%
15	100%

How did you do? In my workshops, the average number of correct responses is 3, or 20%. In other words, most of the college professors I meet do this exercise and come up with a big fat F.

Finding the Pattern in the Words

Now I want you to go back a couple of pages to the words in the box. Read each column carefully, from top to bottom, and see if you can figure out how the words are organized, why one follows the other. Don't take any longer than about 15 seconds to try to work it out. Once your 15 seconds are up, if you still aren't sure, then remove the sheet of paper to read the next page.

The list is organized according to number. Dollar bill represents the number 1 (*one* dollar), dice represents the number 2 (a *pair* of dice), tricycle represents the number 3 (*three* wheels), etc.

Now look at the original list again for 45 seconds. Then come back to this page and list as many of the words as you can remember.

_____   _____

_____   _____

_____   _____

_____   _____

_____   _____

_____   _____

_____

Again, write down the number of items you accurately remembered here: _____

Look back at the table on the previous page for your score and write it here: _____

How'd you do this time? In my workshops, the average number of correct answers for this round is about 12, or 80%. In less than a minute, the participants go from failing to a B–. Pretty impressive.

I do this exercise with audiences in order to convince them of the power of metacognition. It's a way of giving people an experience of how a very simple change can make a profound difference in performance. Now we'll take a look at exactly why our second attempt at the exercise was so much more successful than our first. There are two reasons.

Why It Worked, Reason 1: Clear Expectations

First of all, you actually knew what you were supposed to be doing the second time around! You knew you needed to focus on memorizing the words. The first time, you were on totally the wrong track because I told you to count the vowels.

It may be difficult to believe, but students end up on the wrong track all the time even though their teachers don't purposely mislead them. For example, let's say a teacher assigns chapter 5 of a history textbook as homework. Some students interpret that to mean that they should run their eyes over the reading while they simultaneously text three of their friends. Those students are, figuratively speaking, counting vowels. But when students *know* what active reading involves, then they can get on the right track. That's why I offer multiple strategies in chapter 6 for getting the most out of reading assignments.

Why It Worked, Reason 2: Building on What We Already Know

The second thing that improved your performance is that you started to relate the list of words to something you were already very familiar with: numbers. Learning is much easier when the information we want to learn is related to something we already know very well. In fact, that's actually our only option. We have to relate to new ideas from the context of ideas that we already have. It's why misunderstandings are so common—everyone experiences dozens of them per day—and also why those misunderstandings often require good listening and critical thinking skills to clear up.

Once I was working with a student—let's call him Jonathan—trying to understand why he was having trouble learning the difference between a solid, a liquid, and a gas (like ice, water, and steam). Well, to him, *gas* meant the gasoline he filled his car with, so in his mind, gas was a liquid. Once I explained to him that in chemistry gas has no fixed shape or volume, I showed him how to avoid similar confusion in the future, and his grades rose, no problem. You'll learn in chapters 4–6 exactly what I told him.

But can you imagine if I had made Jonathan feel embarrassed that he didn't know the difference between a gas and gasoline? If I had shamed him for not knowing something I had decided he should already know? In that moment, I had the power to convince him either that he wasn't cut out for science or to help him clear up his own confusion and grow into an expert, skillful learner. We all face that kind of choice on a regular basis: to write someone off as a lost cause or to cheer on their efforts and help them grow. When people choose the first option, so much talent and potential is lost, and those who start out with the least access to academic achievement remain shut out.

Metacognition helps students figure out how to effectively and accurately relate incoming information to the stuff they already know. Then they can do for themselves what I did for Jonathan that day. That's why metacognition has such enormous power to turbocharge a learner's growth and give *all* students the opportunity to excel, including your child.

Metacognitive Learning Strategies

Now that you know what metacognition is, I can tell you that a *metacognitive learning strategy* is just a learning strategy that involves metacognition. That's it. Nothing fancier than that. As I explained in the Introduction to this book, I don't believe there are students who are smart and students who are not smart. I believe there are students who are using metacognitive learning strategies (whether or not they're aware of it) and students who are not.

Applying Metacognition

The next few chapters will enable your child to put metacognition to work for them. Chapter 4 will introduce the idea of lower and higher learning levels, which some students like to compare to lower and higher levels of a video game. Chapter 5 will give your child a special study system to reach higher learning levels, and chapter 6 will give them 10 metacognitive learning strategies to deepen their learning and raise their grades.

Using the Script

As I mentioned in chapter 1, I've prepared a script for you to deliver this information to your child. At the beginning of each script there's a list of everything you will need for that particular section of your session with your child, as well as an estimate of how long it will take. In the body of the script, what you should say to your child appears in regular text. Directions you should follow appear in italicized text in brackets.

You are free to stick closely to the scripts, reading them to your child with as much heart and meaning as you can, or just use the script summaries to structure a more free-flowing conversation with your child.

Please don't just skip to the script summaries, though. The script gives you all of the details your child should hear so it's important to read it through, even if you don't use it when presenting to your child. (But I don't expect or want you to learn the scripts by heart. If you still feel unsure after reading the scripts, there are recordings on the website of me reading each script. You won't play these for your child, but it could help you absorb the information in the script and give you more confidence to deliver it.)

Getting Your Child on Board: The Importance of Buy-In

The very first handout—Handout 3.1: Who is Dr. McGuire and Why Should I Care About What She Says?—introduces me to your child. The handout tells the stories of Jennie and David, the two high school students you met in the Introduction, who got very fast results with the learning strategies. It also gives the before-and-after scores for some of my other students, as well as a short biography. The purpose of this handout is to get buy-in from your child and to make them understand how much confidence I have in their ability to succeed.

Why is it so important to set the stage like this? I'll tell you a story. Once, not more than a few years after I had started giving presentations about learning strategies, I faced a really tough crowd of students. By that point, I was used to open faces, nodding heads, and lots of participation, but this bunch was worse than the audience at the Apollo, one of the toughest rooms in America. After it was over and I tried to figure out what had gone wrong, I realized that, in wanting to save time, I had left out my opening slides showing how previous students had gone from getting Ds and Fs to getting As and Bs. That's when I realized how important it is to let students know that this stuff works *before* I tell them about it.

I have also found that it makes a huge difference to students when they know that an experienced educator has confidence in their ability to succeed. That's why I want your child to feel like they know who I am and that I am rooting for them. A friend of mine puts it like this to her students who struggle with confidence: "Until you believe you can be successful, believe the people who *do* believe you can be successful." And I firmly believe your child can be successful. I know you do too.

On the next page begins your script about metacognition.

Script—Chapter 3: Metacognition

LIST OF MATERIALS:

- Cellphone or other timer
- Pen or pencil
- Script and/or Script Summary
- Handouts 3.1–3.4 to give your child
- Answer Key 3.4A for you to use from the book

ESTIMATED TIME: 10–20 MINUTES

SCRIPT:

Today I want to introduce you to Dr. Saundra McGuire, a learning expert who has some ideas about how you can have more fun with your schoolwork. For almost 50 years, she has been showing students how they can start to enjoy learning and get better grades. Here's a handout that tells you about some students she has helped and also about her life.

[*Hand your child Handout 3.1: Who is Dr. McGuire and Why Should I Care About What She Says? Highlight the overnight jump in Jennie's and David's test scores and the fact that Dr. McGuire has helped failing students become A students. Watch the intro video on www.studyandlearn.guide and peruse Dr. McGuire's short biography together.*]

The main idea that Dr. McGuire uses to help so many students is something called *metacognition*. It's a word that just means *thinking* about thinking. In other words, it's taking a step back from your automatic thinking processes and shining a light on them so that you can have more awareness about *how* you are thinking. With that extra awareness, you can improve the ways you think and solve problems.

In other words, it's like there's a big brain outside your brain looking at what your brain is doing. The big brain helps you think about your own thinking and have more ideas about how to solve problems. It also helps you decide whether you've really learned something deep down inside or just kind of halfway learned it.

[*Hand your child Handout 3.2: What is Metacognition and How Can It Help Me?*]

Take a minute to look at this handout. Then, whenever you're ready, please read the text just under the image out loud.

[*Your child will read the caption of the image on Handout 3.2.*]

What does it mean to think about your own thinking? You can read some words from the handout if you want to.

[*Your child's answer should resemble the ideas in the caption. If they use some text from the four-part definition, that is also fine.*]

What is the more sophisticated word for thinking about our thinking? [*Answer: metacognition.*]

Yes, it's metacognition. Now please read me the four-part definition of metacognition on the handout.

[*Your child will read the four-part definition of metacognition on Handout 3.2.*]

OK, so now let's think about an example. Two people are each trying to find their way out of a maze by themselves. Taylor doesn't know about metacognition, so she can't think about her own thinking. But Alex knows about metacognition, so she *can* think about her own thinking. We're going to consider how Taylor and Alex might have different experiences. You just told me that metacognition gives someone the ability to recognize that they can solve problems by themselves. So sitting there, lost in the maze, how would Taylor and Alex each feel? Remember, Taylor can't use metacognition, but Alex can.

[*Wait for an answer like, "Alex would know she can get out by herself, but Taylor would feel scared because she might doubt that she could do it without help." If your child is stumped, lead them toward this answer or a similar one. Or just give them the answer.*]

You also told me that metacognition gives someone the ability to decide *how* to think through a question or problem. And then they can change their approach if what they're doing isn't working. How might this part of metacognition make Taylor's and Alex's experiences different?

[*Wait for an answer like, "Taylor would just have to wander around and make the same mistake a bunch of times, but Alex could keep track of the things she's doing that aren't working and try different things." If your child is stumped, lead them toward this answer or a similar one. Or just give them the answer.*]

Finally, you told me that metacognition is the ability to accurately judge how well you've learned something, or to accurately judge how well a process is going. How would this part of metacognition help Alex to get out of the maze faster than Taylor?

[*Wait for an answer like, "Taylor might think that she's really close to getting out of the maze when she's not at all, so she might make the same mistakes over and over without even realizing it. Alex would be more aware of how lost she actually is and use a better system for keeping track of different times she tried to get out." If your child is stumped, lead them toward this answer or a similar one. Or just give them the answer.*]

Great! Now that you know what metacognition is, let's do an exercise.

[*At this point, you have the option to play the* Count the Vowels video *for your child and skip to page 28 to, "What do you think made the difference..." If you prefer to lead your child through the exercise, continue reading, but please* also *watch the video to get a sense of how the exercise flows.*]

Here's a pen/pencil, and I've got a timer. I'm going to give you a sheet of paper, and you'll have 45 seconds to count all the vowels in the words that you see on the paper.

[*Hand your child only the first page of Handout 3.3: Count the Vowels and let the timer run for 45 seconds. Then take that page back and hand them the second page of Handout 3.3: Count the Vowels—Recall.*]

Now write down as many of the words as you can remember.

[*Ask your child to compare their list to the original list and count how many they got right. Use the table on page 20 to find their score.*]

In Dr. McGuire's workshops, the average score for this part of the exercise is 3, or 20%. So people don't do too well with this task.

Now look at the original list on the first page I gave you and see if you can work out how the words are organized. Read each column from top to bottom. Do you see any kind of pattern?

[*Let your child look for the pattern until they get bored or frustrated. If they don't see it, explain it to them.*]

The list is organized by number. Dollar bill is for 1 because it's one dollar. Dice is for 2 because there are two dice in a pair. Tricycle is for 3 because there are three wheels on a tricycle. Do you see it? [*Keep explaining until you are sure your child sees the pattern.*] Now I'm going to give you 45 more seconds to study the list.

[*Make sure your child is looking at the first page of Handout 3.3:* Count the Vowels *and let the timer run for 45 seconds. Then hand them the third page of Handout 3.3: Count the Vowels—Recall #2.*]

Now try again to write down every word you can remember.

[*Again, have your child compare their list of answers to the original list, and count how many they got right. Use the table on page 20 to find their new score.*]

In Dr. McGuire's workshops, the average score for this part of the exercise is 12, or 80%. So people are able to go from an F all way to a B in just a few minutes.

What do you think made the difference for her workshop participants and for you? I'll give you a hint. There are at least two things.

[*Wait for your child's answer. It should be something similar to (1) I knew what I was actually supposed to do, memorize the words instead of counting the vowels, and (2) I had a way to actually help me memorize them because of the numbers. They may also come up with other plausible reasons. Make minor changes to the following text based on whether you are affirming your child's correct answer, leading them to a more correct answer, or revealing the correct answer to them.*]

Yes, the first reason you were able to improve your performance is that you knew you were actually supposed to be memorizing the words. The second reason is that you understood how the list was organized, and that helped you memorize it much more efficiently. You used something you were very familiar with—numbers—to help you memorize unfamiliar words. In other words, you had a place to start, and you knew exactly how to proceed and what to do. You weren't just trying random things and hoping for the best.

The point of this presentation is that I will be sharing strategies with you that will help you know what to do when you're studying and trying to learn difficult material. It will help you with that feeling of being lost that everyone gets when they're trying to learn something unfamiliar. That's what metacognition does. It helps us figure out where we are and where we need to go.

Great job! Now you know what metacognition is and how it can help students do much better with their schoolwork. We're going to talk through a worksheet so we can really make sure you've got this down.

[*Give your child Handout 3.4: Metacognition Worksheet, and go through it together conversationally, question by question. Use Answer Key 3.4A to make sure your child's answers are correct.*]

END OF SCRIPT

Script Summary—Chapter 3: Metacognition

LIST OF MATERIALS:

- Cellphone or other timer
- Pen or pencil
- Script and/or Script Summary
- Handouts 3.1–3.4 to give to your child
- Answer Key 3.4A for you, either to print out or just use from the book

ESTIMATED TIME: 10–20 MINUTES

SUMMARY:

1. Introduce Dr. McGuire and the purpose of this session.

2. With Handout 3.1, introduce the rapid, dramatic results that my method can get, watch my introductory video on www.studyandlearn.guide, and help me get buy-in from your child.

3. Introduce the concept of metacognition (Handout 3.2). Have your child give its definition and four aspects. Use the maze analogy to help your child understand how metacognition can help them.

4. Do the Count the Vowels exercise with your child (Handout 3.3) or play the video for them.

5. Review the two reasons that the second recall attempt was so much more successful: (1) You knew what the task was and (2) You had a familiar system for organizing the information. Explain that the point of your presentation is to share some strategies that will help make their schoolwork easier just like memorizing the words got easier.

6. Have your child do the metacognition worksheet (Handout 3.4) and discuss it either after they do it by themselves or while they are doing it, in a conversational way. Refer to Answer Key 3.4A.

Chapter 3 Handout Breakdown

All handouts except the answer keys are available on the website. The table in this breakdown shows all chapter 3 handouts. **The handouts also reproduced in the book are shown in bold.**

NAME	TITLE
Handout 3.1	Who is Dr. McGuire and Why Should I Care About What She Says?
Handout 3.2	What is Metacognition and How Can It Help Me?
Handout 3.3	Count the Vowels
Handout 3.4	Metacognition Worksheet
Answer Key 3.4A	**Answer Key for Metacognition Worksheet**

Handouts 3.1–3.4 are only available on the website.

They are not crucial for understanding the book's content as you read it, but you will use them during your sessions with your child and may want to know what they contain. If so, go to www.studyandlearn.guide.

Answer Key 3.4A, which includes the questions on Handout 3.4, is on the next page.

ANSWER KEY 3.4A Answer Key for Handout 3.4

Answer Key for Metacognition Worksheet

1. What is a three-word definition of *metacognition*?

    Thinking about my/your own thinking

2. What are the four parts of the more in-depth definition of *metacognition*?

    1) The ability to think about my own thinking.

    2) The ability to recognize I have the power to solve problems by myself.

    3) The ability to decide *how* to think through a question or problem. As a result, I can change my approach if what I'm doing isn't working.

    4) The ability to accurately judge how well I have learned something.

3. Choose the four things that the term *metacognition* describes:

    The term *metacognition* describes:

    1) Thinking, "Hmm, I don't think I understand the themes in this book that my English teacher assigned. I'd better have a closer look."

    2) Thinking about my friend's thinking.

    3) A cartoon of a big brain watching a smaller brain do push-ups.

    4) Being able to stop in the middle of solving a problem and go in a different direction.

    5) Being able to figure out how to answer a question by myself.

    6) Spending five minutes studying geometry proofs and deciding I'm ready for the test even though I was really confused in class during the entire unit.

    7) Asking my teacher to help me with something before I've thought about how to do it.

    8) Thinking about my own thinking.

    Correct answers: 1, 4, 5, and 8

    2 would be correct if it said "my own thinking" instead of "my friend's thinking."

4. Review the four parts of the definition of *metacognition* on Handout 3.2. Then explain how metacognition can help a student be more independent.

    If I have the power to solve problems myself, then I can solve more problems without others' help. OR other valid answers.

5. Explain how metacognition can help a student be more creative in their problem solving.

    If I can decide how to think through a problem and to change how I'm doing it whenever I want to, then I can come up with more ways and possibilities to solve it. OR

    If I can see how I'm thinking, I can see other possible ways I *could* be thinking. OR

    If I can change my thinking, that means I have more possibilities for how to solve a problem. OR other valid answers.

6. Explain how metacognition helps students become more confident.

    If a student can come up with more ways to solve problems by themselves, then that will make the student feel much more confident. OR

    Thinking about my own thinking will give me more ideas. OR

    Knowing that I can change course if something isn't working helps me feel confident. OR

    Checking whether I've really learned something will help me to learn it better, and that makes me feel more confident. OR other valid answers.

7. Have you ever had the experience of believing you did well on a test, an essay, or a project only to get it back with a terrible grade at the top? (This has happened to Dr. McGuire, both of her children, and countless students she knows.) Explain how metacognition might help prevent surprises like that in the future. If you need a hint, see the fourth part of the definition of *metacognition* on Handout 3.2.

    Metacognition can help me think about how well I've learned something, so I won't think that I've got something down when it's really still fuzzy in my mind. OR other valid answers.

8. Do you believe that failing the first test in a class means a student is not capable of making an A in the class? Why or why not?

    If the answer here isn't, "No, they can still make an A if they use metacognition to do better on future assignments and tests," then remind them of the results that Dr. McGuire has gotten with other students and her pep talk in the middle of Handout 3.1.

Get to Higher Levels of Learning

Congrats! You're Doing It.

You have just successfully visualized teaching your child about metacognition using handouts and worksheets.

Using the Scripts to Deliver Information to You

In the previous chapter, I explained metacognition to you directly before giving you the script for your child. But in this chapter and the next three after it, I'm going to save us both some time. I'll present the script for you to use with your child and, *simply in reading the script on your own*, you will absorb the information you need to give your child. In other words, you'll be envisioning what to do with your child *and* learning the information at the same time.

Again, there are web-only handouts that the script refers to, but all of the information in those handouts appears here in the book. It's up to you whether you'd like to go to the website while you read the script or wait until you are actually preparing for your sessions with your child.

Of course, you still have the option to use the script summaries during the actual sessions you'll have with your child. Another option is to use a combination of the scripts and script summaries. If you decide to stick to the scripts—a great choice to ensure accuracy—you need not try to memorize them. Just read them directly from the book with warmth and feeling.

A Step-by-Step Method for Introducing Bloom's Levels of Learning to Your Child

At this point in the process, your child will understand what metacognition is. Yet they probably still won't have a feel for what it means to think more deeply or what the phrase *critical thinking* means. Bloom's Levels of Learning[3] will give them that understanding—that ability to tell whether they are thinking in a shallow way or a deeper way. It will enable them to *see* the changes in their thinking and study habits that they need to make.

The box just after this section of text shows a summary of my step-by-step method for introducing students to Bloom's Levels of Learning, which I sometimes shorten to "Bloom's." You'll understand the details as you read through the script. It's basically: (1) a series of questions for your child to reflect on, (2) an explanation of Bloom's, and (3) a final pair of questions.

There are no right or wrong answers to the questions. Yes, there are answers that most students give, and there are answers that might go more smoothly with the script, but there are no wrong answers. No matter how your child answers the questions, you will be able to get them to the same place of understanding in terms of how they can think and learn more deeply. The most important thing is that your child thinks about the questions and answers them as honestly as possible. Whenever a student gives me an unexpected answer in a workshop, I always respond with genuine interest and curiosity, and I never, ever imply that they are wrong or have made a mistake. Because they haven't!

Six-Step Method for Introducing Bloom's Levels of Learning

1. **Ask:** How would you describe the difference between studying and learning?
2. **Ask:** Up until now, have you been operating in *study* mode or *learn* mode?
3. **Ask:** Would you study harder to make an A on a test or teach the material to the class?
4. **Ask:** Up until now have you been in *make-an-A* mode or *teach-the-material* mode?
5. **Present:** Bloom's Levels of Learning
6. **Ask:** Before now, which level of learning have you mostly needed to be at? In your current classes, which level of learning do you mostly need to be at?

A Note About the Script

Toward the end of this chapter's script, there is an exercise based on the children's story "Goldilocks and the Three Bears," which is routinely done with high school and college students. If you or your child don't know the story, this section contains a summary of one version of it. In the script, when you get to the exercise, take a couple of minutes to relay the story to your child before going through the exercise.

Goldilocks is a young girl wandering through the woods. She comes across a house and finds the door unlocked, so she goes inside. She sees a table with three chairs and three bowls of porridge, or oatmeal. Goldilocks is hungry, so she tries the biggest bowl of porridge, but it's too hot. She tries the middle-sized bowl, but it's too cold. The third and smallest bowl is just right. After finishing the porridge, Goldilocks wants to sit down. She tries the biggest chair, but it's too big. She tries the middle-sized chair, but the legs are too short. The smallest chair fits her just right. Then Goldilocks gets sleepy, goes upstairs, and finds a room with three beds. She tries the biggest bed, but it is too hard. The medium-sized bed is too soft. But the smallest bed feels just right, and Goldilocks falls asleep. Just then a family of three bears returns to the house. Seeing the table, Papa Bear, the biggest bear, exclaims that someone has been eating his porridge. The middle-sized bear, Mama Bear, exclaims that someone has been sitting in her chair. The smallest bear, Baby Bear, wanders upstairs and exclaims that someone is sleeping in his bed. Goldilocks wakes up, sees the bears, and runs frightened out of the house.

Script—Chapter 4: Bloom's Levels of Learning

LIST OF MATERIALS:

- Script and/or Script Summary

- Handouts 4.1–4.6 to give your child

- Answer Key 4.6A for you to use from the book

ESTIMATED TIME: 15–20 MINUTES

SCRIPT:

Now that you understand what metacognition is, we're moving on to the next topic. I want you to think about a question and answer it as honestly as you can. There are no right or wrong answers to this question. I just want to know about your experience.

[*Hand your child Handout 4.1: Answering Reflection Questions.*]

OK, here's your first question: How would you describe the difference between studying and learning? You can talk through your answer before you write it down, if you want to.

[*Wait for your child to answer, and then hand them Handout 4.2: Other Students' Answers to Reflection Question #1.*]

Here are some other students' answers to that question. Please read them out loud to me. [*The answers are here for your reference, but your child should read them from their handout.*]

- Studying is memorizing information for the exam; learning is when I understand it and can apply it.

- Studying is short-term; learning is long-term.

- Studying is like being force-fed a plate of yucky food; learning is like standing in front of a buffet and being able to pick my favorite foods.

- Studying is what I do the night before a test to get a good grade. Learning is what I do if I know I'm going to have to use that information later on.

- Studying is focusing on the "whats," but learning is focusing on the "hows," "whys," and "what ifs." If I focus on the "whats," then I often forget them. But if I focus on the "hows," "whys," and "what ifs," then I can recreate the "whats." For example, if I memorize history dates, then I don't remember them. But if I know the context, then I can figure out the dates. Or if I try to memorize the locations of ancient cities, I have trouble. But if I remember that cities are located near waterways because of transportation needs, then that helps me to remember where they are.

[*If it feels right, discuss your child's answer and how it compares to other students' answers—remembering that there are no wrong answers. Otherwise, keep going with the script.*]

So, many people think of studying as more of a shallow, short-term thing, and learning as a deeper, long-term thing. However, it is common for students to answer, "Studying is when I go over what I've learned in class." But there's a difference between learning *about* a topic and the kind of deep, thorough learning that will stick with you long after a test. So, using the definitions of studying and learning you see on the Handout 4.2, here's your second question: Up to this point, have you been operating more in *study mode* or *learn mode*? Please tell me your answer and then write it down on the sheet titled "Answering Reflection Questions."

[*Wait for your child's answer.*]

Most students say that they've been in study mode, so we're going to talk about a way for you to get into *learn mode* and stay there. If you're already in *learn mode*, we're going to talk about how to get even deeper into it.

Now here's your third question: Which of the following two tasks would you work harder for? To make an A on a test? Or to teach the information that's going to be on the test to your entire class without using any notes? Write your answer down on the worksheet. You can talk it out first if you need to. After you've finished writing, please explain why you chose your answer.

[*Wait for your child to answer, and then hand them Handout 4.3: Other Students' Answers to Reflection Question #3.*]

Most students say that they would work harder to teach the whole class. Please read those answers out loud to me. [*The answers are here for your reference, but your child should read them from their handout.*]

- Well, I have to really know it if I have to teach it!
- If I'm going to teach it, I have to think of questions I might be asked and make sure I can answer them. I don't want to look stupid in front of the class.
- I want to make sure everybody understands and is prepared for the test, so I need to figure out how to explain the information in more than one way. I might need to make charts or diagrams.

[*At this point*, if your child answered "teach the whole class," please skip ahead *to "Now for your fourth question!" on page 37.* But if your child answered, "make an A," then give them Handout 4.4.]

But some students do say they would work harder to make an A. Here are a couple of answers from those students. Please read those answers out loud to me. [*The answers are here for your reference, but your child should read them from their handout.*]

- Well, if I want to make an A, I need to master all the angles. So I would read all of the information several times, do all of the problems at the back of the chapter, and re-work any problems I missed on previous quizzes. But to teach it, I would just have to make outlines and read from some notecards.

- It's my grade, so I'm going to care more about it than everyone else's grades.

The student who gave the first answer is actually on the right track because they want to "master all the angles." But students who give an answer like the second one usually change their minds when they hear how other students would prepare to teach the material to the class.

Now for the fourth question: Until now, have you been in *studying-to-make-an-A* mode or *teach-the-material* mode? Please tell me your answer and then write it down under all your other answers on Handout 4.1.

Most students say that they've been in *make-an-A* mode, but after this exercise, they can see that being in *teach-the-material* mode usually leads to deeper learning, as long as they want to make sure that all the students they're teaching get As. The good news is that it's really easy to get into *teach-the-material* mode. You don't need a whole class full of students. You just need an empty chair, a stuffed animal, an action figure, or even just empty space full of imaginary students. No matter how you choose to do it, *you can practice teaching the information that you want to learn.*

Let's talk more about why being in *teach-the-material* mode works so well. Have you ever been in the middle of explaining an idea or a concept from one of your classes that you thought you understood really well, and then you got stuck?

[*Wait for answer.*]

Well, if you hadn't found out *then* that you didn't fully understand it, when would you have found out?

[*Wait for answer.*]

A lot of students say that they would have only found out during the test, when it's too late to do anything about it.

Now we're going to talk about another way of grasping what the difference is between *make-an-A* mode and *teach-the-material* mode. It's called Bloom's Levels of Learning, and it shows how learning goes from lower, shallower levels to higher, more profound levels.

[*Hand your child Handout 4.5: Bloom's Levels of Learning. Have them take one to two minutes to look at it, and then ask them to explain it to you, level by level. It's fine if they basically read it to you. For example, "Level 1 is Remembering, or recalling basic facts and concepts. Level 2 is Understanding or being able to explain ideas or concepts...." Give them a hand if they get stuck.*]

Now let's take an example and try to apply Bloom's Levels of Learning to studying the story "Goldilocks and the Three Bears." Even though it's a children's story, this example is often used with college students.

[*Hand your child Handout 4.6: Bloom's Levels of Learning—Goldilocks Edition. If your child is unfamiliar with the story, relay the summary given earlier in the chapter.*]

Starting from the bottom level and going to the top level, tell me the learning level, the task written on the level, and why the task fits the level. For example, you would say, "For Remembering, I have to list the items that Goldilocks used at the Bears' house. That makes sense because it's just a matter of memorizing or knowing that she used their porridge bowls, spoons, chairs, and beds."

[*Go through the rest of Handout 4.6 with your child. Urge them to consult Handout 4.5 if they get stuck. See Answer Key 4.6A for ideas.*]

Now that you understand metacognition *and* Bloom's Levels of Learning, it's time for the last two reflection questions. First, tell me what level of learning you have mostly been operating at, up to now. Please write your answer down for question #5 and then share it with me.

Now tell me what level of learning you think you need to be operating at in order to do as well as you want to do in all of your classes. Please write your answer down for question #6 and then share it with me.

[*As long as their answer to question #5 is higher than their answer to question #6, you're good to go. If for some reason it's lower, ask them to explain their answers. Then gently guide them in the right direction.*]

It's a really big deal that you can see the difference between where you are right now and where you need to be. High five! Most students who have done this exercise also needed to go to higher learning levels, so you're in good company. Next, we're going to talk about how to use something called the Study Cycle to get to the higher learning levels.

END OF SCRIPT

A Final Word to You, the Parent, About Bloom's

It is possible to do tasks at higher level of Bloom's without mastering the basics. For example, some students can *create* (level 6) a battery out of a lemon without having *memorized* (level 1) the formulas for any positive or negative ions. If your child raises this objection, reassure them that they are not wrong. However, most of the time, higher levels of learning do build upon the lower levels, so Bloom's is still a very useful way of looking at learning, even if it doesn't always apply.

Script Summary—Chapter 4: Bloom's Levels of Learning

LIST OF MATERIALS:

- Script and/or Script Summary

- Handouts 4.1–4.6 to give to your child

- Answer Key 4.6A for you to use from the book

ESTIMATED TIME: 15–20 MINUTES

SUMMARY:

1. Ask: How would you describe the difference between studying and learning? Share other students' answers. (Handout 4.1, Handout 4.2)

2. Ask: Have you been in *study* mode or *learn* mode? Explain that you're going to show them how to get into *learn* mode and stay there. (Handout 4.1)

3. Ask: Would you work harder to make an A on a test or teach the material to the whole class without any notes? Share other students' answers. (Handouts 4.1, 4.3. Possibly Handout 4.4)

4. Ask: Have you been in *make-an-A* mode or *teach-the-material* mode? Explain that they can get into *teach-the-material* mode immediately by pretending to teach to an empty chair, an imaginary class, or even a stuffed animal or action figure. (Handout 4.1)

5. Present Bloom's Levels of Learning (Handout 4.5) as a way of understanding the difference between *make-an-A* mode and *teach-the-material* mode. Have your child explain the handout to you.

6. Present Bloom's applied to "Goldilocks and the Three Bears" (Handout 4.6). Have your child tell you the learning level, the task written on the level, and why the task fits the level. Have them use Handout 4.5 for guidance. Refer to Answer Key 4.6A.

7. Ask: What level of learning have you mostly been operating at up to now?

8. Ask: What level of learning do you think you need to be operating at in order to do as well as you want to do in all of your classes?

9. Make a big deal out of the fact that they can see the difference. Then tell them that the Study Cycle is the way to go to higher learning levels and that you're about to tell them about it.

Chapter 4 Handout Breakdown

All handouts except the answer keys are available on the website. The table in this breakdown shows all chapter 4 handouts, and **the handouts also reproduced in the book are shown in bold**.

NAME	TITLE
Handout 4.1	Answering Reflection Questions
Handout 4.2	Other Students' Answers to Reflection Question #1
Handout 4.3	Other Students' Answers to Reflection Question #3
Handout 4.4	Alternative Answers to Reflection Question #3
Handout 4.5	**Bloom's Levels of Learning**
Handout 4.6	**Bloom's Levels of Learning: Goldilocks Edition**
Answer Key 4.6A	**Answer Key for Exercise with Handout 4.6**

Handouts 4.1–4.4 are only available on the website.

They are not crucial for understanding the book's content as you read it, but you will use them during your sessions with your child and may want to know what they contain. If so, go to www.studyandlearn.guide.

Handout 4.5 appears on the next page.

HANDOUT 4.5   Bloom's Levels of Learning

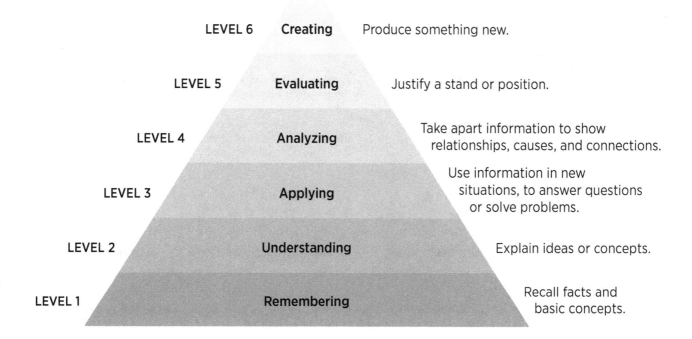

This diagram of Bloom's Levels of Learning goes from the lowest level, *Remembering* (or memorizing), to the highest level, *Creating*. The text in the boxes to the right of the levels explains what each level involves. You can see that the requirements get tougher as you go from bottom to top. Many of my students approach reaching higher levels of learning the way they think of reaching higher levels of a video game. It's fun!

HANDOUT 4.6   Bloom's Levels of Learning—Goldilocks Edition

Example

Bloom's Levels of Learning

Applied to
"Goldilocks and the
Three Bears"

Creating   **Write** a story about Goldilocks and the Three Fish.
How would it differ from Goldilocks and the Three Bears?

Evaluating   **Judge** whether Goldilocks was good or bad.
Defend your opinion.

Analyzing   **Compare** this story to reality.
What events could not really happen?

Applying   **Demonstrate** what Goldilocks would use if she
came to your house.

Understanding   **Explain** why Goldilocks liked Baby Bear's chair
the best.

Remembering   **List** the items used by Goldilocks while she was
in the bears' house.

Adapted, and used by permission, from *Practicing College Learning Strategies* by Carolyn H. Hopper (Cengage Learning, 2015).

ANSWER KEY 4.6A Answer Key for Handout 4.6

Answer Key for Exercise with Bloom's Levels of Learning—Goldilocks Edition

These answers are just suggestions, to give you an idea of what you're looking for. Any answer that makes sense and that your child can justify is great!

1. For Remembering, I have to list the items that Goldilocks used at the Bears' house. That makes sense because it's just a matter of memorizing or knowing that she used their porridge bowls, spoons, chairs, and beds.

2. For Understanding, I have to explain *why* Goldilocks liked Baby Bear's chair most. That makes sense because I need to *understand* that she didn't fit Papa Bear or Mama Bear's chairs, but Baby Bear's chair fit her best.

3. For Applying, I have to say what Goldilocks would use if she came to my house. That makes sense because I have to *use* what I know about Goldilocks in a totally new situation. So, I would have to figure out what things in *my* house would fit Goldilocks, based on the fact that she fits Baby Bear's stuff, and pick those things.

4. For Analyzing, I have to compare the story to reality. That makes sense because Handout 4.2 says that analyzing shows "relationships, causes, and connections." So I have to look at the relationship between the story and reality to be able to say that bears don't have houses in the woods where they're using spoons and sleeping in beds.

5. For Evaluating, I have to judge whether Goldilocks was good or bad and defend my opinion. That makes sense because this level means having an opinion and justifying it. I think Goldilocks was bad because she broke into someone else's house and basically stole their stuff.

6. For Creating, I have to write a story called "Goldilocks and the Three Fish" and say how it would be different from the original story. That makes sense because according to Handout 4.2, creating means to produce something new.

The Study Cycle

The Study Cycle

Like the previous chapter, this chapter consists mostly of a script. The idea is that, as you read through it on your own, you will put yourself in your child's place and learn the material as you are reading it. Please remember that I don't intend for you to memorize the scripts. When you sit down with your child, you can simply read the script aloud with energy, or use the script summary provided at the end of the chapter to have a more free-flowing discussion.

I want to make sure you know how transformative the Study Cycle can be for students. Some of them say that it's the *one thing* that turned their grades around. They started learning faster, and their confidence skyrocketed.

Script—Chapter 5: The Study Cycle

LIST OF MATERIALS:

- Script and/or Script Summary
- Handouts 5.1–5.3 to give to your child

ESTIMATED TIME: 5–10 MINUTES

SCRIPT:

We just talked about the need to move higher on Bloom's pyramid. Now we're going to talk about how you can use the Study Cycle to do that.

[*Hand your child Handout 5.1*]

There are five steps in the Study Cycle. They are:

1. Preview what's coming up in class for 5 to 10 minutes, at some point before class.

2. Go to class.

3. Review what you did in class for about 10 minutes as soon as you can after class.

4. Study the material actively and in depth.

5. Check to see how well you've learned the material you studied.

And then you start from the beginning and do it all over again for the next class. That's why it's called a *cycle*.

Now we'll talk about the first step, *previewing*. You'll do an exercise when we get to the next chapter's materials that will show you how powerful previewing can be. For now, just know that it involves skimming your reading assignments or other class materials, so that you'll be able to understand much more of what goes on in class. Your brain likes to have a big picture before it considers details.

The great thing about previewing is that you shouldn't spend very much time doing it—only five to ten minutes. You can do it at home the night before or, if you have a break just before a class, you can do it immediately before class starts.

If your teacher does not give reading assignments or announce class topics in advance, then you can do this step of the Study Cycle by looking over your class notes from the previous day or two, as well as the most recent materials your teacher has given you.

The second step in the Study Cycle is to go to class alert and ready to participate. Many students think they can miss class and just get notes from a friend later. But it's much better to be in class where you can hear the material firsthand from the person who will create your tests. When you participate in class alert and prepared, you can also ask any questions as they come up, take better notes, and store up goodwill with your teacher.

The third step in the cycle is to review *as soon after class as you can*. Why is that important? Well, have you ever seen a movie twice?

[*Wait for answer.*]

Have you ever noticed that the second time you watched it, you saw things that you didn't see the first time?

[*Wait for answer.*]

That's why reviewing is powerful. When you review, you always catch things you missed the first time. On top of that, you can flag everything you still have questions about and focus on those areas during your study time. Then if it's still not clear, you can take those questions to your teacher, a tutor, or maybe even a friend who is doing well in the class.

If you rarely have breaks between classes, then review as soon as you have the opportunity. It could be at the end of the day, just before a sports practice or rehearsal, before or during a study hall, or at the end of lunch if you finish eating early. Five to ten minutes is often enough time to review one class period of material.

The fourth step of the Study Cycle is to actively study the material, in *learn mode*, and the fifth step is to check to see how well you learned the material you just studied. There are lots of ways to check how well you've learned something, including pretending to teach it to an empty chair or going through a stack of flashcards. We'll look at other strategies and tools in the next chapter's materials.

Here's a way of saying each step of the Study Cycle with only one word, so you can remember it more easily: Preview, Class, Review, Study, Check

[*Refer to Handout 5.1 and ask your child to repeat back to you the steps of the Study Cycle and explain what each step is for.*]

During the fourth step of the Study Cycle, you're going to do something called a *Focused Study Session*. During these sessions you will use metacognition and the learning strategies you'll learn about in the next chapter's materials.

[*Hand your child Handout 5.2.*]

There are five parts to a Focused Study Session. They are:

1. Set specific goals.

2. Use effective learning strategies.

3. Take a break.

4. Review what you studied before the break.

5. Decide whether to keep going, switch to another subject, or take a longer break.

Here's a way of saying each part of a Focused Study Session with one word so that it's easier to remember: Plan, Learn, Break, Recap, Choose

You can see on the handout that you have some flexibility about how long your Focused Study Sessions are. Depending on how much time you have and the way your attention works, you can do a shorter session, an intermediate session, or a longer session. If you have a shorter attention span, or if you only have a limited amount of time, then use the shorter durations. If you have more time or a longer attention span, then use the longer durations.

You should try to aim for having as many Focused Study Sessions per day as you can manage without getting burned out or losing sleep.

Now I'd like you to explain to me the different parts of a Focused Study Session and what they are for.

[*Listen as your child uses Handout 5.2 to explain Focused Study Sessions.*]

Now please circle every type of session—shorter, intermediate, and longer—on the handout that you think you can use. You could use a shorter one while waiting for a bus or for an event to start, and you could use a longer one at home, in the library, or in study hall. You might circle only one or all three. No one option is better than another. It's all about what works for you. Which ones did you circle and why?

[*Listen to your child's answer. Even if you have opinions about it, try to keep them to yourself for now.*]

The Study Cycle is a powerful tool that many teachers have used to help thousands and thousands of students. Some of those students say that it's the *one thing* that turned their grades around.

Now that you know about metacognition, Bloom's levels of learning, and the Study Cycle, you're ready to hear about the learning strategies you're going to use during your Focused Study Sessions.

[*If you want to, and you have your child's approval, take Handout 5.3—which simply shows the Study Cycle and Focused Study Sessions together—and put it on your child's wall or the refrigerator before moving on to the next chapter.*]

END OF SCRIPT

A Note About Previewing

If your child's teacher does not assign readings, announce topics in advance, or give out readings before they are used in class, your child could go to the teacher privately and make a polite request. Your child should explain that they are interested in previewing class material and then ask whether the teacher would mind writing on the board the topics that will be discussed in class the next day. If the teacher declines, your child should graciously accept their response and simply do the Preview step of the Study Cycle by reviewing the notes and materials they have access to.

Script Summary—Chapter 5: The Study Cycle

LIST OF MATERIALS:

- Script and/or Script Summary

- Handouts 5.1–5.3 to give to your child

ESTIMATED TIME: 5–10 MINUTES

SUMMARY:

1. Give your child Handout 5.1 and introduce the five steps of the Study Cycle with the language in the script.

2. Go a little deeper into each step.

   a. Briefly explain that previewing shouldn't take a long time, and that you'll explain it in detail when you get to the next chapter's materials. Explain that previewing is skimming reading assignments and other class materials. Say that the brain likes to have a big picture before it considers details. Explain that if no other material is available, do the Preview step of the Study Cycle by looking over notes and materials from the previous day or two.

   b. Briefly explain why it's important to go to class, using the three reasons in the script.

   c. Briefly explain why reviewing is important (you notice more things the second time around, like seeing a movie twice; you can flag areas of confusion and follow up during study time and also with teachers or tutors). If your child rarely has breaks between classes, explain that they should review as soon as they have the opportunity, and list the options given in the script, in addition to any others you and your child can come up with together.

   d. Say that the fourth step is *actively studying* the material *in learn mode*.

   e. Give your child examples of ways to check their own learning (teaching to empty chairs, going through flashcards, or using other study tools that you'll go over in the next chapter).

3. Go over the easy-to-remember, one-word Study Cycle steps (Preview, Class, Review, Study, Check).

4. Ask your child to explain Handout 5.1 to you.

5. Give Handout 5.2 and introduce the five parts of a Focused Study Session using the language in the script.

6. Go over the easy-to-remember, one-word Focused Study Session steps (Plan, Learn, Break, Recap, Choose).

7. Explain the three different durations of Focused Study Sessions, and that your child should do as many sessions as they can without getting exhausted or sleep deprived.

8. Have your child explain Focused Study Sessions to you, and have them circle, on Handout 5.2, which duration(s) they feel are right for them.

9. Give my strong recommendation to use the Study Cycle and congratulate your child on being ready to hear about learning strategies.

10. If you want to, and you have your child's approval, take Handout 5.3 and put it on your child's wall or the refrigerator for easy reference.

Chapter 5 Handout Breakdown

All handouts except the answer keys are available on the website. The table in this breakdown shows all chapter 5 handouts, and **the handouts also reproduced in the book are shown in bold**.

NAME	TITLE
Handout 5.1	**The Study Cycle**
Handout 5.2	**Focused Study Sessions**
Handout 5.3	The Study Cycle and Focused Study Sessions Combined

HANDOUT 5.1   The Study Cycle

Use the Study Cycle to get the most out of in-class time and structure your out-of-class time.

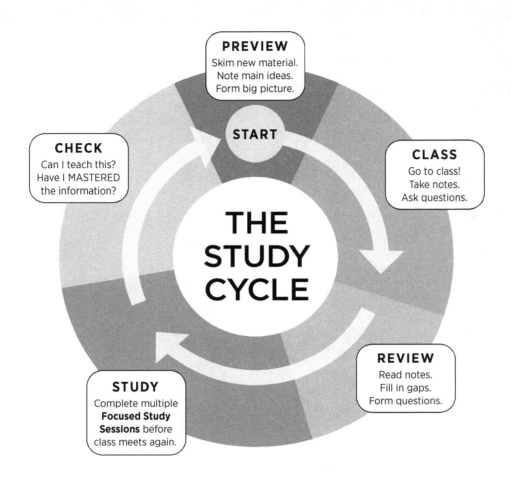

Adapted from Frank Christ's PLRS system.

HANDOUT 5.2 | Focused Study Sessions

FOCUSED STUDY SESSION

Schedule as many study sessions as needed to master the material.

PLAN
1–2 minutes

▸ Set a specific goal.

LEARN
15–45 minutes

▸ Use metacognitive learning strategies to deeply engage with the material by using concept maps, reading for comprehension, working problems and more.

▸ Remember to think critically by asking: *Why? How? What if?*

BREAK
2–10 minutes

▸ Step away. Clear your mind.

RECAP
2–5 minutes

▸ Summarize. Wrap up.

CHOOSE
1–2 minutes

Continue studying?
Take a longer break?
Change tasks or subjects?

SHORTER

PLAN
1 minute

LEARN
10–15 minutes

BREAK
0–2 minutes

RECAP
2 minutes

CHOOSE
1 minute

INTERMEDIATE

PLAN
1–2 minutes

LEARN
25 minutes

BREAK
5 minutes

RECAP
5 minutes

CHOOSE
1–2 minutes

LONGER

PLAN
1–2 minutes

LEARN
45 minutes

BREAK
10 minutes

RECAP
5 minutes

CHOOSE
1–2 minutes

Adapted from Frank Christ's PLRS system.

Handout 5.3 is only available on the website.

It is not crucial for understanding the book's content as you read it, but you will use them during your sessions with your child and may want to know what they contain. If so, go to www.studyandlearn.guide.

Ten Learning Strategies

The 10 Strategies

Here is a list of the learning strategies you will introduce to your child with this chapter. You might notice that the first four—almost half—are reading strategies. That's because your child's ability to learn and securely understand written material is all-important. If you look at this list and think, "Really? I've seen all this stuff before," then stay with me.

1. Preview your reading assignments

2. Come up with questions the reading might answer

3. Put what you are reading into your own words

4. Use the right study tools to understand reading assignments

5. Use homework to test your understanding

6. Be the teacher

7. Participate in class and take notes

8. Go for 100% understanding

9. Use the Study Cycle with Focused Study Sessions

10. Study with a friend or two (optional)

As in the previous two chapters, you'll be learning the information as you read through the script, with the option to view the web-only handouts on the website as you go. As usual, any handouts crucial for comprehension are reproduced here in the book. When you teach the strategies, it's your choice whether to use the script, script summary, or a combination. But I recommend using the script for this chapter, only because there are a lot of details that can make a big difference in understanding the strategies.

Script—Chapter 6: Ten Learning Strategies

LIST OF MATERIALS:

- Script and/or Script Summary

- Handouts 6.1–6.5 to give to your child

ESTIMATED TIME: 30–35 MINUTES

SCRIPT:

I'm going to tell you about 10 learning strategies you can use to feel more confident and successful when you study. You don't have to use *all* of them, but I think you'll see how most of them are helpful. You can think of the first four as a four-part strategy for reading. We'll begin by exploring what usually happens when we read.

When most of us begin to read anything that isn't just for fun, we usually only get through a few sentences before our mind starts to wander. We don't instantly realize we're not paying attention because our eyes are still going over the text and the words are washing over us, even as we're thinking about something totally different. Only when we're halfway down the page do we realize, "Oh I'm not getting this at all." Has that ever happened to you?

[*Wait for answer.*]

If you're like many students, then after you realize you stopped paying attention, you go back and re-read, but you only get a little further before your attention wanders again. You drag your attention back to the page, but before you know it, your mind has gone somewhere else, *again*. After a few more rounds of this, maybe you get tired of trying so hard to focus your attention. Maybe you feel lost, despite your best efforts, and you decide that the reading is too hard to finish. Maybe then you give up entirely. Has that ever happened to you?

[*Wait for answer.*]

The following reading strategies I'm going to tell you about are designed to break you out of that pattern so that you can get the most out of your reading assignments.

Learning strategy #1 is called Previewing. Previewing is looking through a reading assignment and paying attention *only* to headings, bold and italicized words, and any pictures or images. It should only take you five to ten minutes.

Now I'm going to give you a handout that has a paragraph for you to read, and I want you to try to figure out the activity that it's describing. I'll give you about a minute.

[*Hand your child Handout 6.1: Guess the Activity, **page 1 only**, and give them about a minute to read it.*]

Okay, now have a look at the same paragraph, but with a heading.

[*Hand your child Handout 6.1: Guess the Activity,* **page 2***, and give them about a minute to read it. If your child happened to guess the activity correctly, then you can emphasize how* much *faster and easier* it is to understand with the title heading added.*]

Once the heading is added, it's a lot easier to tell what's going on in the paragraph, right? That's the power of previewing. When you know what you're about to read, or what you're about to hear about in class, it's much easier to make sense of, and you can catch a lot more details. That way, you learn the material faster and better. Did you ever notice that when you learn a new word, you start hearing it everywhere? That's not because the word is actually being said or written more often. It's because, before you knew the word, your brain just filtered it out as nonsense. Once you learned it, then you could see and hear it. Previewing before you go to class and before you do your reading assignments helps you actually *see and hear* more information than you would otherwise.

Learning strategy #2 is to Come Up with Questions the Reading Might Answer. Your brain doesn't like to be forced to do things. You need to fire up your curiosity so that you will *want* to read. One way to activate your brain's interest is to ask yourself questions that you think the reading assignment might answer. For example, if you're reading about the American Revolution, you might ask yourself questions like, "When did that happen? How long did it take? Was it before or after the French Revolution? How violent was it? Were there any disagreements about strategy? Spies or double agents?"

Or let's say you're reading a chapter in your chemistry textbook about acids and bases. During your previewing, you see the terms *strong acid* and *weak acid*, so you might ask yourself, "What makes an acid strong? What makes it weak?" That way, you give your brain a reason to want to do the reading.

Learning strategy #3 is to Put What You Are Reading in Your Own Words. Imagine you're supposed to read a chapter from your history textbook. If you decide to use strategy #3, you begin by reading the first paragraph and then summarize it in your own words—you *paraphrase* it. You could do it out loud, or just in your head. Next, you read the second paragraph and summarize that paragraph in your own words *as you also fold in information from the first paragraph.* Next, you read the third paragraph and summarize that paragraph in your own words *as you also fold in information from the first two paragraphs*. Then after you read the fourth paragraph, what would you do?

[*Wait for answer like "summarize that paragraph in your own words as you also fold in information from the first three paragraphs." If your child hasn't picked up the pattern, go ahead and read this section of the script again and help them to see it.*]

You repeat this process until you reach the end of the section, and then you start fresh at the beginning of the next section. This strategy helps you understand each section of reading *as a whole* instead of just separate bits of unrelated information. It helps you move up to higher levels on Bloom's pyramid.

Learning strategy #4 is to Use the Right Study Tools to Understand Reading Assignments. As you are using the third reading strategy, you'll also want to use the study tools that are right for you. Maybe you'd like to make flashcards for terms, dates, and ideas that you need to memorize and understand. Maybe you'd like to highlight particular phrases or sentences, perhaps using sticky notes or tabs if you're not allowed to mark up your reading material. Or maybe you enjoy making mind maps, or concept maps, of an entire chapter, showing how different concepts relate to each other. Timelines are another great tool. You'll get a handout at the end of this session that lists several useful study tools. See which ones you enjoy using the most.

If you find it distracting to write anything down *while* you are reading, you can always wait until you've gotten to the end of a section, or a whole chapter, to start making your flashcards, maps, or notes—as long as you have been doing your paraphrasing all along the way. Of course, if it works better for you to write things down as you read, then do it that way, using whichever tools fit your study style. Do you have any favorite study tools right now?

[*Give your child an opportunity to list some study tools they use. But if their answer is no, feel free to move on.*]

And if you are interested, there is also a packet available that explores a range of study tools in detail. [*The packet is Appendix B: Study Tools Guide.*]

Combining the four reading strategies that we just talked about will help you get the most out of your reading assignments and have much more fun while you learn. Then you'll be able to do your best on all your quizzes and tests.*

The next learning strategy—**strategy #5**—is how so many of Dr. McGuire's students went from making Cs, Ds, and Fs to making As and Bs. They started **Using Their Homework to Test Their Understanding**. Let's start digging into this strategy by thinking about how most people do their homework.

When Dr. McGuire asks students how they do their homework, most of them say that when they're trying to answer a question or work a problem, they flip to an example in their book, or a handout from the teacher, and follow along with the example to try to answer the question. Can you relate to that?

[*Wait for answer.*]

---

* This method has many similarities with the SQ5R reading method—Survey, Question, Read, Recite, Record, Review, and Reflect. If one of your child's teachers is using that method, or one similar to it like SQ34 or SQ4R, there is no need to replace it with the one described here unless it is more effective for your child.

Although following along with examples is an extremely common way to do homework, it's not the best way.

Instead, you should study your notes and reading assignments as well as you can *before* you turn to your homework. While you are studying, if you come across any example problems or end-of-section questions in your reading assignments, then you should do those. But it's important that you make sure to try them *without* looking at the solutions first. We'll talk about how to do that in just a minute.

Once you've thoroughly studied your notes and reading assignments, and you've worked through any sample questions or problems you came across while reading, you're going to close the book and your notes. *Now* you turn to your homework and do the assigned questions or problems without looking at your notes or reading. That way, you discover how well you have learned the information by seeing how well you are able to apply it. If you approach your homework using this method, then every single time you do homework, you'll be training yourself to ace your next test.

[*Hand your child Handout 6.2: Using Homework to Test Your Understanding.*]

Look at the section of your handout titled, "Procedure for doing problems or questions without looking at notes or solutions." It lays out *exactly how* to do example questions in your reading or questions in your homework assignments. You should use this procedure for both kinds of questions. Begin the question or problem by just focusing on the first step. It might be the first step of a math or science problem, the first step in outlining an essay question, or the first step in designing a process for a woodworking or lab class. Whatever kind of task you're trying to do, you'll want to focus on *just the first step*.

Set a timer for three minutes and do your best thinking and brainstorming until the timer goes off. If you finish the first step before three minutes is up, move on to the second step. If you're not done with the first step after the timer goes off, but you're making progress, then reset the timer for another three minutes and keep going. Reset the timer as many times as it takes for you to finish that first step, or until you get stuck.

If at any point you get thoroughly stumped for a whole three minutes, or you just can't take it anymore, then go ahead and look at your notes, but only the notes that help you solve *that first step*. Then, once step 1 is done, move on to the second step. Do it exactly the way you just did the first step.

After you've finished the second step, move on to the third step, and keep going until you finish the question, problem, or process.

It might seem kind of scary or intimidating to think about answering a question without having anything to look at or rely on. So, the first thing to do is to recognize that the feelings of uncertainty, doubt, or even worry are perfectly normal. It doesn't mean that anything is wrong. Plus, if you let yourself feel those feelings while you're doing your homework, then you won't have to feel them during the test, right? Usually, the earlier we face our fears, the better. Whenever you feel unsettled, take a few deep, slow breaths. That usually helps.

Now I'd like to hear from you. Why do you think this strategy helps students learn better?

[*Give your child about a minute to throw out some ideas. If they simply shrug their shoulders, you can either prompt them or just move on to the next part of the script. Feel free to adjust the next part of the script depending on how closely it matches your child's ideas.*]

The idea behind this strategy is that you are training your brain to work exactly the way it needs to when you're taking a test. If you do your homework this way, it will teach you that even when you're convinced that you can't remember anything or don't know how to do anything, you can probably come up with *something*. And the more you practice coming up with *something*, the easier it will be to come up with what you need during a test.

So, to review this strategy, you're going to:

1. Study your notes and reading assignments.

2. If you come across example problems or sample questions as you study, do them *without* looking at your notes or the reading. If you get stuck, break the question down into steps, and use a three-minute timer to help you decide when to keep thinking and when it's okay to take a look at your notes.

3. After you've finished studying the notes and reading, put them away. Then do your homework problems or questions *without* looking at them. Again, if you get stuck, break each question down into steps, and use a three-minute timer to help you decide when to keep thinking and when it's okay to take a look at your notes.

4. If you start to feel unsettled or worried at any point, remember that those feelings are normal, and take a few deep, slow breaths.

Using your homework to test your understanding also gets careless mistakes out of your system. Have you ever gotten a test back and thought, "Oh, I would have done so well if only I hadn't made so many careless mistakes?"

[*Wait for response.*]

Well, what if there are no such things as careless mistakes and they only look that way in hindsight? Once you know what the right answer is, then your simple mistakes *look* careless. But mistakes have to be made. It's part of the learning process. For example, you might hastily multiply 6 times 8 and come up with 24 instead of 48. Or, on a multiple-choice test, you might choose 1963 as the year that the Emancipation Proclamation took effect, instead of 1863, because you weren't reading carefully enough. When you make mistakes like these as you are doing your homework, then you can figure out *why* you made them and avoid them in the future. But if you don't make mistakes by using your homework to test your understanding, then when are you going to make them?

[*Wait for response. The answer you expect is "on the test." You can respond, "Exactly."*]

Now we'll move on to **learning strategy #6**, which is another strategy that many students say helped them pull up their grades. We've already talked about how trying to teach something to someone else helps us learn it more deeply and securely. So strategy #6 is to *Teach* **Whatever You Are Trying to** *Learn*. You can teach to an empty chair, a stuffed animal, your reflection in the mirror, an action figure, an imaginary class, or whatever you want.

It can be very powerful to combine this strategy with the previous one. Page 2 of Handout 6.2 explains how to do that: First, you study your notes and reading. Next, you teach that material to an empty chair (or whatever you want) until you can do it confidently. Then you use your homework to test your understanding in exactly the way we just talked about.

Learning Strategy #7 is to Participate in Class and Take Notes. When we learned about the Study Cycle, we talked about the fact that going to class is important because you learn the material directly from your teacher and you're able to ask questions as they come up. Taking notes in class is also very important. It keeps you engaged with what the teacher is doing, and it gives you something to review after class, so that you can do step 3 of the Study Cycle. Don't try to write every single word down, but instead try to pick out the most important points and write those down in your own words. If the teacher works through problems or examples on the board, be sure to also write those in your notes. Remember that you can also make doodles or sketches in your notes, if it feels easier to you to represent the information with images instead of words.

Learning Strategy #8 is to Always Strive for 100% Understanding. Have you noticed that however hard you try, you usually do a little bit less well than you wanted to? Can you think of an example of when that has happened to you?

[*Take less than a minute to listen to your child's experience or, if they are stumped, share your own.*]

Well, that's normal. It's part of being human. Most of us underestimate what it takes to achieve a goal. It's not because we're foolish or because something is wrong with us. It's just because that's just how most of our brains work. It's sort of like how it's hard to stay on a skateboard unless you practice. Most people fall off. But if we *know* we tend to underestimate what effort is needed, then we can make up for that by trying to do even more than we think we should. So, if you try your hardest to learn 100% of all of the information you're being taught, then you know you're going to do the very best you can.

But there's another, more important reason you should always aim for 100% mastery. Learning always builds on previous learning. The more you learn in ninth grade, the more you're *able to* learn in tenth grade. So, if you start going for 100% mastery now, then by the time you graduate from high school, you could be miles ahead of where you would have been if you hadn't aimed for 100% mastery.

This is also true across subjects. For example, ninth grade history can help with tenth grade English. Physics or chemistry can help with aviation school or cosmetology or college philosophy. The more you learn, the better you'll be at learning, and the more readily you'll be able to do the things you want to do in life. And that's the real reason I want you to go for 100% mastery: so that you can do whatever you want to do and make the most of your life, hopefully having as much fun as you can while you do it.

[*Here you could have a short back-and-forth with your child about some of the things they want to do or create. There is also an exercise in Chapter 11 that asks your child to explore their dreams and goals.*]

Let's keep going. We're almost done. **Learning Strategy #9 is to remember to Always Use the Study Cycle with Focused Study Sessions**. When students start doing better with learning strategies, sometimes they fall back into their old ways because they stop using the Study Cycle. Their higher grades lull them into a false sense of confidence, and they start to wing it. But if you want to keep your learning deep and your grades up, always use the Study Cycle with Focused Study Sessions.

Learning Strategy #10 is to Study with a Friend or Two. Many students enjoy having a couple of study buddies. But there are pros and cons to this approach. Can you think of some advantages and disadvantages of studying with others?

[*Give your child a minute or less to throw out some ideas. Feel free to adjust the following text according to how closely it matches your child's ideas. And if they shrug their shoulders, no problem. Just continue with the script.*]

When you study with friends, you can go back and forth between doing some Focused Study Sessions quietly on your own and then doing other ones together, teaching each other the material and quizzing each other. You can also hang out and have social time during your five- to ten-minute breaks. But you have to know yourself. Are you likely to play around with your friends, and then you *all* do badly on your test? Or can you keep yourself on track and use the time together for learning?

[*Wait for answer. Discuss for a minute or less, if appropriate.*]

OK, *great* job. Now that you've learned about Dr. McGuire's 10 learning strategies, you're ready to do a worksheet to deepen your understanding. Here's a handout summarizing the 10 strategies and a worksheet that you can work through out loud with me or on your own for 10 minutes.

[*Hand your child Handout 6.3: Ten Learning Strategies and Handout 6.4: Learning Strategies Worksheet. Work through the worksheet together or give them time to think through it and then discuss it together. All the answers can be found in this chapter's script.*]

Awesome work. You've absorbed a lot today. Like I promised earlier, I'm just going to give you a quick list of study tools for you to hold onto, but you don't have to read it now unless you want to. You can ask me any questions later.

[*Hand your child Handout 6.5: Quick Reference: List of Study Tools.*]

END OF SCRIPT

Additional Info for Parents: Study Tools Guide

Appendix B at the back of this book expands upon the list of study tools in Handout 6.5. It lays out several different kinds of study tools in detail over roughly 20 pages, with examples, figures, and extended explanations. If your child begins to regularly do their Focused Study Sessions and you sense that they need more ideas about how to study, have a look at Appendix B: Study Tools Guide. As long as you think that it will not overwhelm your child, you can print it out and give it to them. But don't do it until you have finished presenting all of the material in Chapters 3–11. If you do give them the Study Tools Guide, you can go over it together or to let them read it independently. It is addressed directly to students. Chapter 12 includes instructions on how and when to introduce this packet of tools.

Please be aware that Appendix B is pitched at a higher level than the rest of the book. It is aimed at students currently grappling with the subject content used in the examples. So parts of Appendix B may be difficult for the average parent, who probably hasn't thought about meiosis, trigonometric identities, literary analysis, or states of matter in decades. Justifiably so! But the Appendix is designed to go a little deeper for students who need that extra challenge. If it's not right for your child at the moment, maybe it will be in a year or two. In the meantime, the Study Cycle and the learning strategies should keep them busy and successful.

Peyton's Story

I want to share with you a story from a teacher who works at a school where I shared my system of learning strategies with both teachers and students. I've changed the names to protect everyone's privacy. I hope it will inspire you to believe that no matter how your child is doing in school right now, they can turn things around. Feel free to share this story with your child if you think it will inspire them.

Email from Mrs. Rinaldi at Oaks Glen School:

> I have been awed by the impact of Dr. McGuire's talk. The common language the Oaks Glen community has gained from her talk has allowed both teachers and students to identify the distinction between "learn mode" and "study/memorization mode." My conversations with students are more meaningful and I'll share the results of one of those conversations. I'll refer to the student as Peyton.
>
> Peyton has been struggling in the first-year physics class since the beginning of the year, despite attempts to help her by the school counselor and me. Shortly after Dr. McGuire spoke to the first-year students, Peyton performed poorly on a quiz. She was visibly distraught and was berating herself. We had an opportunity to speak, and she recognized that she has been in "study/memorization mode" and not in "learn mode." I saw an immediate change in her for the rest of the class period and the next day she

scored a 94% on her quiz. She said she is in "learn mode" and is constantly questioning why, even if she has already gotten the "correct" answer.

Script Summary—Chapter 6: Ten Learning Strategies

LIST OF MATERIALS:

- Script and/or Script Summary

- Handouts 6.1–6.5 to give to your child

ESTIMATED TIME: 30–35 MINUTES

SUMMARY:

1. Explain that you will be discussing 10 learning strategies and that the first four are a four-part strategy for reading.

2. Explain what happens when most of us start reading (see script).

3. **Strategy #1: Preview**

   a. Define it: Previewing is looking at all of the headings; bold, italicized, and underlined words; and images like charts, graphs, tables, pictures, or other visual aids.

   b. Remind your child it is step 1 of the Study Cycle.

   c. Do the activity with Handout 6.1.

   d. Explain why previewing increases learning.

4. **Strategy #2: Come Up with Questions the Reading Can Answer**

   a. Explain that the brain resists being forced to do things, so we have to activate our curiosity by asking questions.

   b. Example 1: questions you might ask when studying the American Revolution (see script).

   c. Example 2: questions you might ask when studying strong and weak acids (see script).

5. **Strategy #3: Put What You Are Reading into Your Own Words**

   a. Explain my paraphrasing strategy. Read one paragraph and put it into your own words, either out loud or in your head. Then read the second paragraph and summarize that paragraph in your own words *as you also fold in information from the first paragraph*. Next, read the third paragraph and summarize that paragraph in your own words *as you also fold in information from the first two paragraphs*. Continue until the end of section. Start fresh at the beginning of the next section.

6. **Strategy #4: Use the Notetaking Tools That Are Right for You**

   a. Some options include flashcards, highlighting, mind mapping, outlining, and using charts, graphs, tables, timelines, study guides, or mnemonic devices.

   b. If you find it distracting to write things down *while* you read, you can wait until the end of a section or chapter—as long as you are mentally doing your paraphrasing all along the way. If it's better for you to write things down *as* you read, do that. Which option is better depends on your brain.

   c. Ask your child which study tools they like to use and let them know there's a packet available if they're interested, Appendix B: Study Tools Guide.

7. **Strategy #5: Use Homework to Test Your Understanding**

   a. Describe how most students do their homework (see script).

   b. Outline the method (see script).

   c. Explain how to do problems or questions without notes or reading assignments, using a timer. Use Handout 6.2 so your child can follow along.

   d. Explain how to use deep, slow breathing to deal with any emotions of discomfort.

   e. Review the method in four steps (see script).

   f. Ask your child if they can think of why this strategy helps students learn. Explain how it trains students to ace tests (see script).

   g. Discuss why "careless mistakes" must be made at some point during the learning process (see script for examples).

8. **Strategy #6: Teach Whatever You Are Trying to Learn**

   a. You can teach to an empty chair, invisible students, stuffed animals, an action figure, your own reflection. Whatever works.

   b. Combine this strategy with strategy #5 for a very powerful approach. Study your notes and reading; teach the material; then use your homework to test your understanding (Handout 6.2, page 2).

9. **Strategy #7: Participate in Class and Take Notes**

   a. Going to class is important in order to hear the material directly from the teacher and ask questions.

   b. Taking notes is important because it keeps you engaged in class and gives you something to review afterwards.

c. When taking notes, don't try to write every word down. Instead try to capture the main points and write them down in your own words. Use doodles or sketches if it sometimes feels easier to use images instead of words.

10. **Strategy #8: Always Go for 100% Understanding**

a. Explain that humans tend to underestimate what a task will take, so giving a little bit extra is always a good idea. Ask your child to come up with an example from their life or share one from yours.

b. The better you learn something now, the better you'll be at learning other things in the future (see examples in the script).

c. The main purpose of this strategy is to make sure your life is the most fun and rewarding it can be and that you have the widest possible range of choices.

11. **Strategy #9: Use the Study Cycle with Focused Study Sessions**

a. Sometimes when students start to do better, they fall back into their old ways because they stop using the Study Cycle.

b. But always using the Study Cycle with Focused Study Sessions (Handout 5.3) keeps learning deep and grades up.

12. **Strategy #10: Study with a Friend or Two**

a. Ask your child to come up with some pros and cons of studying with others.

b. Let them know that when they study with friends, they can alternate between doing Focused Study Sessions quietly on their own and doing lively ones together with their friends.

c. Advantages: Making sure everyone is studying, teaching each other the material, quizzing each other, taking breaks together.

d. Disadvantages: Too much social time; not enough studying time.

e. Ask your child whether, if they're honest, they think this is a good strategy for them. If it is, make a list of potential study buddies.

13. Give your child Handout 6.3: Ten Learning Strategies.

14. Together, work through Handout 6.4: Learning Strategies Worksheet.

15. Give your child Handout 6.5: Quick Reference: List of Study Tools, but you don't need to look closely at it.

Chapter 6 Handout Breakdown

All handouts except the answer keys are available on the website. The table in this breakdown shows all chapter 6 handouts, and **the handouts also reproduced in the book are shown in bold.**

NAME	TITLE
Handout 6.1	**Guess the Activity/The Power of Previewing**
Handout 6.2	Using Your Homework to Test Your Understanding
Handout 6.3	Ten Learning Strategies
Handout 6.4	Learning Strategies Worksheet
Handout 6.5	Quick Reference: List of Study Tools

HANDOUT 6.1   Guess the Activity

Read the following paragraph and try to guess what activity the text is describing.

> A newspaper is better than a magazine. A seashore is a better place than the street. At first it is better to run than walk. You may have to try several times. It takes some skill, but it is easy to learn. Even young children can enjoy it. Once successful, complications are minimal. Birds seldom get too close. Rain, however, soaks in very fast. Too many people doing the same thing can also cause problems. One needs lots of room. If there are no complications, it can be very peaceful. A rock will serve as an anchor. If things break loose from the rock, however, you will not get a second chance.

The Power of Previewing

FLYING KITES

A newspaper is better than a magazine. A seashore is a better place than the street. At first it is better to run than walk. You may have to try several times. It takes some skill, but it is easy to learn. Even young children can enjoy it. Once successful, complications are minimal. Birds seldom get too close. Rain, however, soaks in very fast. Too many people doing the same thing can also cause problems. One needs lots of room. If there are no complications, it can be very peaceful. A rock will serve as an anchor. If things break loose from the rock, however, you will not get a second chance.

Do you see that the heading of the paragraph helps you make sense of the text, which probably seemed like nonsense before you read the heading? This exercise gives you an idea of what happens when you take five to ten minutes before class to preview what will be covered in class.

Previewing is taking your assigned reading and looking at all of the headings, bold words, italicized words, underlined words, and images like charts, graphs, tables, photographs, or other visual aids. Knowing that the paragraph on this page is about kites helped you to make sense of it. In the same way, having an idea of what will be covered in class makes it easier for you to digest what the teacher is saying, stay engaged in class, and ask questions as they arise instead of discovering confusion later at home or on a test. *Previewing is powerful! And it only takes five to ten minutes.*

Mindset: Knowing That Your *Actions* Matter Most

The Second Half of This Book—Mindset, Motivation, and Planning—Begins Here

In Chapter 2, I let you know that this book is roughly divided into two parts. You've just finished the *Learning* half, and now we begin the *Mindset, Motivation, and Planning* half. You can think of this part of the book as the key that turns the *Learning* lock.

As always, you have the option to use the script, the script summary, or a combination. Similar to the last chapter, details matter quite a bit here, so using the script is a great choice. I recommend at least having the script at hand. If you opt for the script summary, it is very important to convey the material accurately. All of this chapter's handouts are here in the book, so you can follow along with them as you read the script.

As I also mentioned in Chapter 2, this is the first chapter where I encourage you to actually go through the worksheets on your own before your child does. You don't necessarily have to do it with pen and paper, but it's important to investigate your own attitudes and beliefs about intelligence before you share this information with your child.[4]

Script—Chapter 7: Mindset: Your *Actions* Matter Most

LIST OF MATERIALS:

- Script and/or Script Summary

- Handouts 7.1 and 7.2 to give to your child

- Answer Key 7.2A for you to use from the book

ESTIMATED TIME: 20–25 MINUTES

SCRIPT:

As we go through this chapter's material, we're going to talk about how you can stay motivated when it comes to doing your schoolwork. Having the right frame of mind can make the difference between reaching your goals and giving up on them. Researchers have shown that how we think about our intelligence affects how well we learn.[5]

Consider the following two ways of thinking about intelligence: We can imagine that intelligence is determined when we're born, and that it's unchangeable, sort of like eye color or height. *Or* we can imagine that intelligence is more like cooking ability, and that it has unlimited potential to grow, depending on how much effort we put into it.

[*If another ability, like gardening or playing a sport or an instrument, fits your child better than cooking, then feel free to substitute that ability.*]

A psychologist named Carol Dweck came up with some terms to describe these attitudes. According to her research, people who think of intelligence as something unchangeable have a *fixed mindset*, while people who think of intelligence as something that can grow have a *growth mindset*. If a person has a fixed mindset, they think that their *current ability* matters more than their *behavior*. But if a person has a growth mindset, they think the opposite. They think that *what they do* matters more than *how smart anyone thinks they are*. In other words, they think that the actions they take in the future matter more than what they have done in the past.

[*Give your child Handout 7.1: Fixed and Growth Mindsets.*]

Take a look at this handout contrasting the characteristics of someone with a growth mindset and the characteristics of someone with a fixed mindset.

[*Take as much time as you need to go over Handout 7.1 with your child because the ideas in it are so important. First ask them to define a fixed mindset and a growth mindset. Help them find the definitions at the top of the figure if they're having trouble. Then ask them to tell you some characteristics of a person with a fixed mindset. Do the same for a growth mindset. Look at each set of contrasting characteristics on the figure.*]

By the time you have finished Handout 7.1, the following ideas should have been expressed at some point by your child: People with a fixed mindset tend to avoid challenges, give up easily, ignore criticism, and find the success of others threatening. People with a growth mindset embrace challenges, persevere, use effort to achieve mastery, benefit from criticism, and get motivated by the success of others.]

So you see that there's a big difference between someone with a growth mindset and someone with a fixed mindset. Now let's imagine a student we'll call Anthony, who has transferred to a new high school. He is sitting in history class on the day the teacher hands back the first exam. Up to this point in his life and in his old school, Anthony has always gotten good grades in history and thought of himself as very good at the subject. But when he gets his test back, there's a big red D at the top. Anthony feels confused. The D on the test doesn't match his belief that he's good at history. He feels embarrassed, shoves the test in his bag, and thinks to himself, "I must not be good at history." Have you ever been in a situation like Anthony's? Can you ever remember getting a disappointing grade and thinking that it means something about what you're capable of doing in the future?

[*Wait for answer.*]

Which kind of mindset would you say Anthony has?

[*Wait for answer, which should be: Fixed.*]

What do you think Anthony might have said to himself if he had a growth mindset?

[*Wait for answer. Give your child time. If they are stumped, give them a hint without giving them the whole answer. You can encourage your child to look at the handout and remember what the characteristics of a growth mindset are. Sample answer:* Oh! I thought I had done better than this. I'll look the test over as soon as I can to see where I went wrong. I'm sure if I make some changes to my study habits, I'll do better on the next one.]

Now we're going to look at two examples of how mindset has affected students in the real world. In the first example, a team of researchers compared how two different groups of students reacted to different kinds of feedback on their homework assignments.[6] Students in both groups received critical, negative feedback on their assignments. But students in the first group also received an extra note explaining the purpose of the feedback. The note said, "I have high standards, but I believe you have the potential to meet them, so I am providing this critical feedback to help you meet those standards." Students in the second group did not receive this extra note.

Students in both groups were told that they could use the negative feedback on their assignment to make corrections and hand it in again for a higher grade. But most of the students without the extra note did not make corrections. In other words, the students who *didn't* know that the purpose of the negative feedback was to help them reach their potential didn't try to improve their grades. But most of the students in the first group, the ones who knew that the criticism was intended to help them, *did* make corrections in order to earn a higher grade on their homework. How might you explain that? What do you think each group of students believed about their ability to improve?

[*Listen to your child's ideas about this study. Feel free to adjust the following text based on how closely it resembles your child's ideas. If your child seems hesitant to offer thoughts, gently encourage them to take a guess and then keep going with the script.*]

Many of the students who read the feedback on their assignments interpreted it as a judgment of their *ability*. They had a fixed mindset and didn't see any point in trying to improve. But the students who were told that the criticism was an *opportunity to improve* could see the feedback as a chance to grow. The extra note helped those students get into a growth mindset.

But what about students who already think of themselves as very smart? Does a fixed mindset hurt them? One Louisiana math teacher's experience says yes. Mrs. Valasco taught students who were labeled gifted and was frustrated that they were performing far below their potential. Although she gave them problems she knew they were perfectly capable of solving, they would write "IDK" all over their papers, to her great puzzlement. She asked one of the students, "What does IDK mean?"

"I don't know," one student responded.

So she asked another student, "Do you know what it means?"

"I don't know," the second student answered.

After one more round of this confusion, Mrs. Valasco got frustrated and exclaimed, "If you don't know what IDK means, why are you all writing it on your papers?!"

After the class burst out laughing, someone finally explained to Mrs. Valasco that IDK stands for "**I D**on't **K**now."

But all jokes aside, why do you think these students who had been labeled gifted didn't want to work on the challenging problems they had been given?

[*Listen to your child's ideas. Feel free to adjust the following text based on how closely it resembles your child's thoughts. If your child just shrugs their shoulders, it's fine to keep going with the script.*]

Can you see evidence of a fixed mindset in their behavior? If being smart is just something you *are*, then the minute you have trouble meeting a mental challenge, it threatens the idea that you are smart. These students gave up before they even *started* trying to solve a challenging problem because their fixed mindset prevented them from seeing a challenge as a way to grow. Even Dr. McGuire fell victim to this kind of thinking when she got one bad grade on a chemistry test in graduate school—she changed her major because she was convinced that she wasn't cut out for chemical research, something she knows today is untrue.

So if a fixed mindset is so destructive, why does anyone have one? It all starts when we're very young, the first time we notice kids being sorted into different groups. Perhaps one group was labeled "smart" and another group was labeled "slow." No matter what group a child gets put into, these labels teach us that intelligence is fixed. But in fact, 10 years down the line, someone in the "slow" group could be doing far better than someone in the "smart" group. Unfortunately, though, a lot of people still believe in these fixed categories.

Dr. McGuire once worked with a student at a prestigious college whose dream was to become a brain scientist. Amitha really wanted to do a project with a professor she respected. But when Amitha asked her, the professor replied, "Why do you even think you can be a brain science researcher if you're making Cs in my class?" Amitha went home and cried all night. She thought long and hard about what to change her major to and what else she could do with her life. Then, after reading Dr. McGuire's book, *Teach Yourself How to Learn,* she found out about metacognition and learning strategies, and she made all As the next year. Amitha's professor had grown up with a fixed mindset and was passing it on to her students. But Amitha didn't let that stop her from having a growth mindset and reaching her goals. In fact, Amitha's success made that professor question *her* fixed mindset.

Dr. McGuire herself used to have a fixed mindset, before she saw thousands of failing students turn their performance around using simple learning strategies. That is why she is so passionate about convincing you that you can succeed. So don't worry when you encounter someone with a fixed mindset. You could convince them, with your own success, to adopt a growth mindset instead.

Did you know that your brain is built to learn? It has a quality that scientists call *plasticity*, which is just a fancy way of saying that our brains are moldable, kind of like clay. In other words, our brains can change and adapt, based on the experiences we have. We are always capable of learning new things because our brain cells can make new connections and pathways. In general, the more we practice something, the better we get at it. Those kids you think are so smart? They just regularly *practice* learning, and so they've gotten good at it. You can practice learning too. And the more you do it, the more fun it is to learn. The more fun it is to learn, the more you can learn, and then learning is *even more* fun.

Athletes and performers often have a special insight into mindset because they have direct experience achieving mastery through effort, through practicing and rehearsing. Coaches and trainers all over the world know that someone with average ability who is willing to put in a lot of effort will often do better in the long run than another person with an impressive amount of ability but who coasts on their talent.

[*If your child is an athlete or performer, talk for a minute about how they've seen their abilities grow through effort in those areas.*]

There are endless stories about young people who get the biggest scholarships and most exclusive opportunities but who never manage to find their footing as adults. There are also endless stories about young people who start out at a disadvantage but who believe in themselves, work harder *and* smarter, and end up having very happy lives as adults, enjoying themselves and contributing to the world around them. Talent and ability are far less important than what you *do* with what you have.

You've done a great job learning about mindset. Now we're going to look at a worksheet to make these ideas even clearer to you.

[*Hand your child Handout 7.2: Mindset Worksheet. Work through the worksheet together and skip over any questions that you have already discussed extensively. Most answers are in this script. Answer Key 7.2A gives answers to select questions.*]

High five. Now let's talk about some more strategies to keep you motivated.

END OF SCRIPT

Script Summary—Chapter 7: Mindset: Your *Actions* Matter Most

LIST OF MATERIALS:

- Script and/or Script Summary

- Handouts 7.1 and 7.2 to give to your child

- Answer Key 7.2A for you to use from the book

ESTIMATED TIME: 20-25 MINUTES

SUMMARY:

1. Explain that this chapter's material is about staying motivated to reach our goals. How we think about our intelligence is a big part of that.

2. Introduce the difference between thinking that intelligence is fixed (like eye color or height) or that intelligence can grow (like cooking, or any other ability).

3. Introduce the definitions of *fixed mindset* (that intelligence is fixed) and *growth mindset* (that it can grow).

4. Growth mindset says future action is vastly more important than current ability, and it also says, "what I do is vastly more important than how smart people think I am."

5. Go over Handout 7.1 with a short discussion. Your child should verbalize all of the differences between a growth mindset and a fixed mindset.

6. Give the example of Anthony, a student who has just transferred to a new high school. He thinks of himself as a good student but gets his first history test back with a D. Ask the questions in the script.

7. Explain that you're going to give two examples of students affected by mindset.

   a. Students who receive a note with negative feedback vs. students who don't (see script). Ask your child to explain the difference in the two groups' behavior before revealing the explanation.

   b. Math teacher of gifted students who write IDK (see script). Ask your child to explain the students' behavior before revealing the explanation.

8. Where does a fixed mindset come from?

   a. Sorting very young children according to different abilities.

    b. Tell the story of the college student whose professor had a fixed mindset and thought she wasn't cut out to be a brain researcher because she was making Cs. Then she used learning strategies to get all As and convinced her professor to have more of a growth mindset.

9. People with fixed mindsets can change.

    a. Dr. McGuire used to have a fixed mindset.

    b. Who knows who you might convince to have a growth mindset by using these learning strategies?

10. Our brains can change. They have a quality called *plasticity,* which means they can make new connections and pathways.

11. People who are smart have learning strategies, even if they aren't aware of them. They practice learning all the time.

    a. If you use learning strategies, you can practice learning all the time, too.

    b. Athletes and performers have growth mindsets in their areas of expertise because they see the power of practicing or rehearsing. Coaches and trainers have long known that effort can beat talent.

12. Do Handout 7.2: Mindset Worksheet (check your answers with Answer Key 7.2A).

Chapter 7 Handout Breakdown

All handouts except the answer keys are available on the website. In this chapter however, I consider all the handouts crucial for understanding, so they have all been reproduced in the following pages and therefore shown in bold.

NAME	TITLE
Handout 7.1	**Fixed and Growth Mindsets**
Handout 7.2	**Mindset Worksheet**
Answer Key 7.2A	**Answer Key for Select Questions on Mindset Worksheet**

TWO MINDSETS
CAROL S. DWECK, Ph.D.
Graphic by
Nigel Holmes

Fixed Mindset
Intelligence is static

Growth Mindset
Intelligence can be developed

Leads to a desire
to look smart
and therefore a
tendency to...

Leads to a desire
to learn and
therefore a
tendency to...

CHALLENGES

...avoid
challenges

...embrace
challenges

OBSTACLES

...give up
easily

...persist in the
face of setbacks

EFFORT

...see effort as
fruitless or worse

...see effort as
the path to mastery

CRITICISM

...ignore useful
negative feedback

...learn from
criticism

SUCCESS OF OTHERS

...feel threatened
by the success
of others

...find lessons and
inspiration in the
success of others

As a result, they may plateau early
and achieve less than their full potential.

As a result, they reach ever-higher levels of achievement.

All this confirms a **deterministic view of the world.**

All this gives them a **greater sense of free will.**

Used by permission from *Mindset: The New Psychology of Success* by Carol S. Dweck (Ballentine, 2007).

HANDOUT 7.2 | Mindset Worksheet

1.   Retrieve Handout 7.1: Fixed and Growth Mindsets. Use the information on the handout to fill in the following chart, and contrast the characteristics of fixed and growth mindsets. Which would you rather have?

Characteristics of a Fixed Mindset	Characteristics of a Growth Mindset

I would rather have a _____ mindset because _____

2. Has there ever been a time in your life when you responded to criticism or negative feedback with a determination to improve? _____

    _____

3. Did you improve? _____

4. Has there ever been a time in your life when you decided to give up on an activity that you enjoyed because someone else said you weren't very good at it or gave you negative feedback?

    _____

    _____

5. What was the difference between the activities in question 2 and question 4? Why did you keep going with the first activity? _____

    _____

    _____

6. Before today, would you say you had more of a fixed mindset or a more of a growth mindset?

    _____

    _____

7. True or False: For many students, grades primarily reflect past behavior rather than talent or ability.

    _____

    _____

8. Are grades always a reflection of your potential? If not, what do grades show? _____

    _____

    _____

9. Do you believe your current ability or your future behavior will determine your grades in the future? Why?

    _____

    _____

10. Do you believe you will be smarter in five years than you are right now? In one year? In a month? Explain.

    _____

    _____

11. What is the biological basis of the idea that intelligence can grow? What can brain cells do? _____

    _____

    _____

Answer Key for Select Questions on Mindset Worksheet

The questions that do not appear in this answer key are personal questions that have no right or wrong answers.

1. See Handout 7.1 for answers.

7. True.

8. Are grades always a reflection of your potential? If not, what do grades show?
   No. Grades only show what I have been doing to study and learn up to this point.

9. Do you believe your current ability or your future behavior will determine your grades in the future? Why?
   My future behavior will determine my grades because I can use metacognition and learning strategies to do a better job with my homework and prepare much better for my tests.

11. What is the biological basis of the idea that intelligence can grow? What can brain cells do?
    Plasticity. Brain cells can make new connections and pathways.

Motivation Part 1: Getting Excited to Learn

You already have a major tool for influencing your child's motivation—mindset. But you may need a range of other tools to keep your child's motivation high so that they stay engaged with and excited about schoolwork. Anyone who has ever tried to make lifestyle changes knows that knowing *what* to do is often less than half the battle. Finding the motivation to keep going in the face of obstacles is usually the bigger hurdle. That's why I've devoted two entire chapters to this crucial topic.

Chapters 3–7 laid out the general principles of studying, learning, and mindset, applicable to all students. Chapters 8–10 are all about your specific child, the particular things that will work for them.

The key to unlocking motivation is paying attention to what your child *enjoys*. The main idea here is that we want to find every opportunity to tailor the experience of schoolwork and learning to our children's unique interests, strengths, and weaknesses. In other words, we want the brick house of learning skills that we're building to be able to withstand all kinds of hurricanes, tornadoes, and typhoons. And genuine desire is the only flawless weatherproofing.

If that sounds dramatic to you, you might be surprised how many students' motivation and drive have been demolished by one difficult class, a challenging standardized test, a college application rejection, or an unsupportive adult offering a destructive opinion about their capabilities. But when students are motivated by their own desire and enjoyment, they have more access to the inner resources they need to bounce back from adversity. Whether your child is headed for sunny or stormy weather, this chapter gives you tools and resources to help them get where they want to go.

No Script This Time

The rest of the chapters in this book do not have scripts because the particular words you use will depend so much on your child's personality. Instead, I lay out everything you need to know, tell you the purpose of each of the handouts, and let you know when and how to use them. The rest will be up to you. But, as with all the other chapters, please do read through all of the handouts before sitting down with your child to have your sessions together. While you're reading, you have the option to visit the website and see all of the handouts.

A Worksheet Just for You

During our discussion of mindset, I asked you to think through the worksheets from your own perspective. But this chapter has the only worksheet in the book that's written *just for you*. I designed it to deepen your understanding of how motivation works.

So What Is Motivation?

When a person thinks about doing a task or striving toward a goal, there are three questions that impact their motivation:[7]

1. Do I find this goal important?

2. Do I feel supported in working toward this goal?

3. Do I believe I can make and carry out a plan to accomplish this goal?

If the answer to one of these three questions is no, a person's motivation will suffer. I'm going to tell you what to do to help your child answer yes to all three questions. In other words, I'm giving you tools to help your child find schoolwork meaningful, feel supported in doing it, and believe in their own ability to accomplish it.

What We'll Cover in This Chapter

Here's an outline of the topics in Chapter 8:

- Helping your child answer Yes to "Do I find this goal important?"

  — Connect to your child's genuine interests, dreams, and aspirations. Help them articulate what's important to them (Handout 8.2).

  — Help them distinguish things they love doing from things they love getting praise for doing.

  — Help them form *direct connections* between their ultimate goals and schoolwork they might be having trouble getting motivated to do.

  — Help them understand that meeting *any* challenge makes us better at meeting *every* challenge.

  — Help them understand that we can use our desire to "eat dessert" to motivate us to "eat our vegetables."

- Make sure they feel the power of choice to determine their own future, even as you encourage them and hold them accountable to accomplish tasks they may find difficult or unpleasant.

■ Helping your child answer Yes to "Do I feel supported in working toward this goal?"

   — Know why emotions have been scientifically shown to play a role in learning.

   — Let your child know you value their goals and dreams.

   — Let them know they're not alone.

   — Let them know they have room to make mistakes (see also Chapter 9).

   — Encourage them to seek out their preferences (Handout 8.3).

   — Consider making learning a family affair.

■ Helping your child answer Yes to "Do I believe I can accomplish this goal?"

   — Tell them about metacognition, learning strategies, and mindset (Chapters 3–7).

   — Give them strategies for breaking a task down and figuring out *exactly* what to do (Handout 8.4).

   — Help them to have an encouraging inner voice, rather than a harshly critical one (Handout 8.5).

   — Help them learn how to take responsibility and see what *they* can do to change a situation (Handout 8.6).

■ Using external motivators.

   — Consider using rewards such as screen time and gifts.

   — Keep in mind that your praise is one of the most important external motivators, and praise your child *skillfully*, not counterproductively.

   — Nurture self-compassion rather than self-esteem

■ Actions to take when nothing else is working.

   — What to do when your child has trouble taking responsibility.

   — What to when your child is overscheduled.

   — What to do when your child's skills gap may be too big.

   — What to when your child may have an undiagnosed learning challenge.

   — What to when your child is dealing with trauma.

Helping Your Child Say Yes to Question #1: "Do I Find This Goal Important?"

Your child needs a gut-level connection to the importance of their education. If a subject isn't genuinely important to them in some way, they will have real trouble learning it. Think about the last thing you tried to learn that you had zero interest in. No amount of nagging can make up for a lack of sincere interest. Trying to get most children to do things "because I said so" just does not work in the 21st century. Why? They are exposed to so many distractions that have literally been engineered by some of the smartest people on the planet to hijack their attention. But the good news is that being motivated by curiosity and interest, rather than fear, is actually much healthier for children and leads to deeper learning.

So, use your child's interests as your compass. Take every chance you can to connect to whatever they're into. For example, if they love gaming, why not consider reading a gaming magazine, or even learning how to play? You could ask them to show you their favorite TikToks or other short videos and tell you what they love about them. Stay open and curious during these conversations. The more details you know about the things your child loves, the more creative you can be in helping relate their schoolwork to those interests. If your child loves building things but can't see the purpose of learning history, you could spend 10 minutes on the internet and start dropping interesting historical facts about construction or architecture into your conversations, pointing out how the two subjects are related. Maybe you could even find an interview of someone your child respects talking about the importance of whatever subject they're having trouble with.

Say your child loves being a part of leadership in organizations but can't see the point of trigonometry and is getting a D in the class. You could begin by asking about what organization they would love to lead after high school. Get your child to really visualize that dream in detail—what it looks like, what it feels like, what they are accomplishing, the service to others they are bringing. And then remind them that they can help that dream come true by doing as well in trigonometry as they can, because higher grades will open more doors to them. Then, every time they feel overwhelmed by cosines and secants, they can think back to that vivid, three-dimensional experience of their future self at their dream job—and work harder at their trig grade to help realize that dream.

In fact, I've given you two resources to encourage your child to discover what gets them fired up. Handout 8.2 invites your child to list their interests, and Handout 11.1 is a worksheet that asks them to imagine a future they might like to have. The first part of Handout 11.1 provides a list of values and professional goals that your child can choose an unlimited number of, and it also asks them to write down some dreams and aspirations they may already have. The second part of the worksheet is an optional exercise where they use their imagination to envision a future for themselves. The third part is an optional exercise where they create a vision board (or journal or short film, etc.) depicting the future they want to create for themselves.

What We Enjoy Doing Versus What We Do Well

I just asked you to prioritize your child's interests. But it's also important to understand what is motivating those interests. Generally speaking, human beings are interested in things for one of two reasons, or maybe a combination. Either we love *doing* a thing, or we love something about *what happens* when we do the thing. That could be getting approval, or money, or power, or just the satisfaction of knowing that the thing got done.

When we love *doing* something, even if there are some things about it that we dislike, we can usually always find the energy to do it. But when we only like doing something because of outside factors, then our motivation can suffer if anything about one of those outside factors changes. That's part of the reason I want to instill a deep love of learning in every student. That way, it doesn't matter if there are things about their teachers or school that they don't like—they can still get excited about *learning*.

Let's think about it from a slightly different angle. Is there something in your life that you do well and that people ask you to do all the time but that you hate doing? For me, it's being president of volunteer organizations. I do it because I want the organizations to run smoothly and I hate saying no to people. So, I get the satisfaction of avoiding that unpleasant friction by saying yes, even though I don't enjoy the task.

Now what about something in your life that you love but aren't that great at. In my case, I really enjoy singing even though I'll never be asked to do it professionally. But I would rather belt out my favorite songs in my car than go to a volunteer committee meeting any day.

If those were my only two choices for what to do with my life, guess what everyone would be telling me I should do? Thankfully those were not my only two choices, and of course, a person ideally chooses something to do in life that they enjoy doing *and* are good at. My point here is that it's important to help your child filter out the noise of other people's opinions and locate their genuine interests—the things that get them energized and motivated deep down inside, not just things that get them approval or help them avoid conflict. Those core desires will help to motivate them through the most unpleasant of tasks.

To sum up, it's helpful to try to separate the joy of *doing a thing* from the joy of *getting something for doing that thing*. The first joy—the joy of doing a task—is resilient to criticism and setbacks, but the second joy—for example, the joy of winning or getting approval—is not. Choosing a life path based on the second joy is a recipe for a midlife crisis and depression.

Dana's Story: The Power of Choice

I'd like to tell you a story about Dana. She's a former student of mine who I met at a "Change Your Major" workshop at LSU. This young woman had wanted to be a medical physicist ever since she was 13 years old, but when she received a 54 on her second college physics exam, she was convinced she wasn't cut out for physics. Most people, when they hear Dana's story, reply, "Oh yeah, I get it. Physics is waaaaaay too hard." But I wanted Dana to know that if she ultimately decided to leave physics, she wasn't leaving because she *couldn't* do it. So I spent about an hour with her, giving her the reading, homework, and teaching strategies laid out in chapter 6. On her next physics test, Dana got a 91! And she followed that up with a 97 on the fourth test and a 90 on the final exam. She went on to graduate from LSU with honors and received her master's degree in medical physics from the famous MD Anderson Cancer Center at the University of Texas. Now Dana is a practicing medical physicist, and she loves her life. Despite Dana's initial failure doing what she loved, her commitment and passion fueled her hard work to reach her goal.

But I would have supported Dana even if she had wanted to leave physics to become a puppeteer. In that case, I would have connected that physics to her future life in puppetry. And I would have had at least two options for doing that. First, I could have looked for a way to *directly connect* the physics class to Dana's ultimate desire. If Dana had actually wanted to be a puppeteer, I could have pointed out how useful physics would be for shadow puppetry, where understanding the physics of light would help her realize her creative vision. Second, I could have reminded Dana that getting through *anything* tough helps prepare her for life, no matter what she went on to do. In other words, meeting a challenge in *any* area helps us meet challenges in *every* area. One popular way of expressing this idea is to say, "Polish over here, and it shines over there."

The second option is a trickier sell because we often need to accumulate some life experience to realize its truth, that no effort is wasted. But you can help convince your child of its truth by opening their eyes to the unpleasant things they're *already* doing in order to pursue the things they love. Maybe your sports-crazy kid hates doing laundry but manages to do it so they have a clean uniform at every practice. Maybe your budding e-athlete spends hours with bug-riddled games or finicky Wi-Fi. Maybe your ambassador-in-the-making hates bus rides with a fiery passion but makes the trip to Model United Nations every year. You can call to their attention whatever way your child "eats their vegetables" before getting to enjoy "dessert," and then encourage them to purposefully tie their genuine goals and desires to anything they're having trouble feeling motivated to do, including schoolwork. In fact, there is a worksheet in Chapter 11 that asks your child to relate each of their classes to a life goal.

Helping Your Child Say Yes to Question #2, "Do I Feel Supported?"

The most important word in question #2 is *feel*. How we *feel* about doing a task often determines whether or not we do it. So let's take a look at why feelings affect learning so deeply. Basically, the spot in our brains responsible for reacting to stress is really close to the spot responsible for accessing our memories, both short-term and long-term. Because they're so close, they influence each other. So too much stress and fear can literally prevent us from learning.

For many of us, though, nobody cared how uncomfortable we felt when we were learning. Maybe tactics of fear or threat of punishment were used to motivate us, and we turned out okay, perhaps even *great*. You might be thinking, "Why wouldn't we use the same tactics on our children?" or "Why should I treat my child like a marshmallow? The real world is tough!"

Yes, it is. And that's why people with deep inner confidence and a sense of wholeness show a lot of resilience. Intimidation only works up to a point. Too much stress and fear physiologically stop us from learning. I acknowledge that fear is a powerful motivator and that it's necessary to use sometimes. But using it regularly will eventually negatively affect a person's mental health. Ideally, we want to find the sweet spot where our teens are handling the biggest challenges they can but without going into a stress reaction that is too intense.

The question remains: *How* can they feel supported?

- By knowing that we support their dreams and aspirations

- By knowing it's normal to feel fear and doubt when facing a challenge

- By knowing it's okay to make mistakes

- By knowing it's okay to seek out their preferences

- By feeling that learning is a community effort

Let's look at each of these points.

Supportive Message #1: I Value Your Hopes, Dreams, Goals, and Aspirations

Let your child know that you want them to do as well as they can in every subject because you want them to succeed in whatever *they* want to do. It will free them to do their best. Otherwise, they could, for example, subconsciously (or even consciously) tank their debate performance because they think you want them to be a lawyer. Or they might fail pre-calculus, because their subconscious is protecting them from having to become the doctor they think you want them to be. But if you communicate to your child that you respect their hopes and dreams and just want them to reach their academic potential no matter what they decide to do later, that support from you will free them to connect to a deep love of learning.

Supportive Message #2: You're Not the Only One Feeling This Way. It's Normal.

Struggling people often think that they're the only ones struggling and that everyone else is A-OK. Social media can make this feeling worse. (That's why psychologists often recommend group therapy to people going through challenging circumstances—so they can see that what they're feeling is normal.) But you can try to make sure your child knows that the fear, doubt, and dread they may feel before tackling challenging tasks is perfectly normal. In fact, you can let them know that sometimes you feel it too. Consider sharing with your child the things that you have trouble getting motivated to do. But please make sure the message isn't, "I did it, so why can't you do it?" or "I did it, so you have to do it," but rather, "We're in this together. I know how you feel."

Supportive Message #3: You Have Room to Make Mistakes

Chapter 9 lays out what you can do to help your child feel comfortable with failure and making mistakes. For now, consider how you might share some of your own failures and difficulties with your child. Think about how you might convey the idea that everyone makes mistakes, and that failure is a part of life because it's how we grow and learn. You might also pay attention to how you react to your own mistakes around the household. Do you mutter to yourself under your breath, "Grrrrr. That was so stupid." If so, why not consider trying to take your next mistake lightly and laugh it off instead, focusing on how easy it would be to correct it? Start modeling that it's okay to make mistakes and we don't always have to have all of the answers.

Supportive Message #4: Do What You Prefer Whenever You Can

It's important to do whatever you can to make sure that how your child studies and learns is tailored to *them*—their interests, strengths, weaknesses. Handout 8.3 helps your child articulate their preferences about a number of things, including people, situations, and ways of learning. On that worksheet, I have emphasized that although having a fixed idea of ourselves is not helpful, it is useful to be aware of our preferences for those times when we *do* have a choice. I've asked your child to share the worksheet with you once they've filled it out. If you look carefully at their answers, you can support them in choosing the study conditions and tools that might be the most enjoyable and effective for them. We return to this theme in Chapter 10. Furthermore, the progress-tracking worksheets in Chapter 11 will enable you to see how well particular strategies and study tools are working for your child. If their preferences aren't working for them, you will be able to see that and gently suggest to them that they try other strategies and tools.

Let me just take a moment here to say that I am aware that there is no evidence for learning styles that reaches the scientific standard of proof, which is why I always talk about *learning style preferences* and emphasize that it's important to be open to learning no matter how information is delivered. But it's also true that enjoyment fuels motivation, and so if a student greatly prefers to learn by reading instead of listening, or via images rather than text, then accommodating that preference can help the student learn, just because they are enjoying themselves. Think of it like this: There's no good evidence that some people would get fitter by swimming, others by biking, and others by running. It's all exercise. But fitness coaches always emphasize the importance of choosing an exercise you love *so that you will consistently do it*. That's why I believe there is value in encouraging students to investigate their preferences while being open to learning in every possible way.

Another way you can help your child tune into their preferences is by giving them opportunities to make their own choices. Maybe they can't choose where the family vacation will be, but why not let them plan a half day with the sights they most want to see? We want to give our children a sense of power over their lives so that they feel they have the right to make choices based on their individual preferences. That sense of self-determination will come in handy at school when it's time for them to choose where to sit in class, who to choose for a project partner, or which extra credit projects to take on. The more your child learns to make choices according to what they enjoy instead of what they think will gain the most approval or avoid the most disapproval, the more they will be able to enjoy learning and do well in school.

Supportive Message #5: We're in This Together as a Family

One final way you can make sure your child feels supported is to make learning a family affair. Say your fourth grader is learning about phases of the moon and your 10th grader is learning geography. The latest eclipse or asteroid is in the news. You could have a lively family discussion about how the moon might look from different places on earth. Having the answers isn't important here. The point is modeling curiosity, making connections between school and "the real world," and hearing details from your children about what they are learning. Finding answers together isn't as important as asking interesting questions together.

You could even take turns giving little fun talks about whatever everyone is learning as you're sitting around the dinner table or taking a car ride. You could turn it into a game. The options are endless.

Helping Your Child Say Yes to Question #3: "Can I Actually Do This?"

Now we turn to the third question that impacts motivation: "Do I believe I can make and carry out a plan to accomplish this goal?" There are a few things that can help your child answer yes:

- Having effective learning strategies and a growth mindset (Chapters 3–6)

- Knowing exactly what they should be doing (Handout 8.4)

- Using encouraging self-talk (Handout 8.5)

- Connecting outcomes to causes in a productive way (Handout 8.6)

- Making concrete plans and schedules (Chapter 9)

The first and last bullets are dealt with in other chapters, but we'll address the middle three right now.

Yes-You-Can Message #1: You Can Do It Because You Have Great Learning Strategies and a Growth Mindset

The most important way to make your child feel confident that they can successfully do their schoolwork is to give them the tools to do it: metacognition, the Study Cycle, and the learning strategies. Those nuts and bolts, along with the belief that they can get smarter, are the vital foundation of successful learning.

Yes-You-Can Message #2: You Can Do It Because You Know How to Figure Out Exactly What to Do

A student has to be able to answer the question: "Do I even know what I'm supposed to be doing?" For example, one of my grandsons started failing one of his math classes during the COVID-19 pandemic. When his parents investigated the situation, they discovered that he had been struggling with the steps he needed to take in order to log into the class website and find his assignments. He didn't know what the steps were, and he didn't know how many of them there were. Not knowing exactly what he had to do meant he was sunk before he even got to the subject matter he was supposed to be learning!

"Knowing exactly what to do" is another way of saying "having clear expectations." In the midst of any task or project, we need to be able to answer the question, "What is my next step right now?" in order to move forward. When the answer to that question isn't clear, then trying to complete an assignment can feel like moving through quicksand. It's *especially* true that struggling students need clear expectations.[8] So if your child is having trouble with schoolwork, try to help them understand what is expected of them on a daily basis, and try to make sure they have tools to meet those expectations.

Handout 8.4 at the end of this chapter takes a student through how to figure out exactly what a homework assignment requires by using class materials to ask themselves a series of questions. My intention is that your child will progress from being told what is expected of them to being able to figure it out entirely on their own.

You can also share with your child specifically what *you* expect from them. Many students benefit from knowing that they are expected to do their very best, and it may be useful to state a reasonable grade average your child is expected to maintain. Researchers have found that high expectations are particularly important for struggling students, so if your child is having trouble, be sure to let them know that you expect them to succeed because you know they're capable of it. You don't want to issue a decree like, "4.0 or else!" but I do encourage you to set a target that you are confident your child can meet. There's a worksheet in Chapter 12 designed to help you set clear expectations.

Yes-You-Can Message #3: You Can Do It Because You Know How to Give Yourself Encouraging Self-Talk

Self-talk is just a name for the chatter most human beings have running through their heads. *"Oh, I need to take out the trash....Where did I put my keys?...Argh, socks on the floor again."* When we're trying to solve a problem, this chatter is sometimes directed at ourselves. *"Think...think....OK, now what about if I move this part over there...yeah, that's it...and fiddle with this thing, no...Darn it! Oh, how could you have screwed that up? That was dumb of you...."* It's common for self-talk to be negative because most of us have learned to use fear and negativity as a motivator. But to make learning as easy as possible, self-talk should be encouraging and kind.

You can use Handout 8.5 to help explain self-talk to your child. We don't want working on self-talk to feel fake and awkward, although if someone's self-talk is very negative, it might feel that way at first. One good way to encourage more helpful self-talk is just to spend a little bit of time noticing it every day, maybe while you brush your teeth. If it's negative, just notice how it makes you feel. For some people, just noticing is enough. They don't even have to try to change it. Their brains just realize, "Oh this doesn't feel good at all. I'll choose a kind thought instead." Over time, people often find themselves noticing their self-talk more and having more opportunities to direct kind, encouraging thoughts toward themselves.

The goal is for your child to get to a point where, for example, they can get a bad grade on a homework assignment or quiz and think something like, *"Oh wow, I really did not understand the Krebs cycle, did I? I guess I'll need to spend more time on this later. But I can definitely do this,"* instead of, *"Stupid, stupid, stupid. It's no use. I'll never get this stuff. I might as well stop trying."*

If your family is particularly open, you could make a game out of sharing unintentionally negative self-talk and revising it in the moment. The whole family could play. Maybe you get five points if you say, "Oh, I caught myself being unkind to myself when I spilled the juice just now. But it's easy to clean up and I'll be more careful with the cap next time." And whoever has the most points at the end of the week gets to choose the Saturday night menu.

Yes-You-Can Message #4: You Can Do It Because You Know How to Focus on *Your* Part

Our minds are storytelling machines. They naturally make all sorts of cause-and-effect relationships, all of the time, even if those relationships aren't real or correct. For example, let's say I'm in class and I raise my hand. My teacher knits her brow and calls on a student behind me who put his hand up after I did. I might think, "My teacher didn't call on me because she's mad at me." My brain decided that (a) she knit her brow because she was angry, (b) not only is she angry but she's angry at *me*, and (c) that's the reason she called on someone else. None of those conclusions are valid, but our brains do this all of the time. The thing is, these wacky conclusions often affect our future behavior. I might never raise my hand in that class again, and that decision will affect how much I learn and the grades I get.

I often use the following example with students, and it appears on Handout 8.6. Let's say I get caught out in a rainstorm without my umbrella. I have some choices for *how* to explain why I got wet. I could say, "Oh, the stupid weather!" or "Why didn't Professor Smith tell me that it was raining?" Or I could say, "Oh dear, I forgot my umbrella. I'll make sure to stick a Post-it note on my computer reminding myself to take it next time." Do you see the two options? I can blame factors *outside* my control, or I can focus on things *within* my control. Notice that I don't blame or judge myself for forgetting the umbrella. But I do take responsibility for what I could have done to ensure a different outcome.

When things don't go your child's way—whenever they experience disappointment or failure—it can make a huge difference if they understand how to *explain* that disappointment to themselves by focusing on things that they can control. Handout 8.6 teaches them how to do that. Part of this worksheet asks them to list three disappointments and, for each of them, give three contributing factors out of their control and three contributing factors within their control. Then it asks them to consider what they might have done to bring about a different outcome.

When discussing these ideas with your child, it's important to make it clear that taking responsibility for our part of a situation does not mean that others have no responsibility in it. It's just that our part is the only part we can control, so if we want to feel the most motivated, that's the part we focus on. (Make sure your child understands that people who are behaving abusively should be called to account; I do not want to encourage anybody to look past or swallow others' inappropriate behavior by trying to change themselves. Sometimes it is critical to focus on another person's part in a situation. At those times, we should do that without hesitation and with vigor and clarity.) Focusing on our own part in a situation has the most power to move us forward.

Other Kinds of Motivation: Screen Time, Gifts, and Other Rewards

By now you know how important I think it is for a student to be motivated by their own desires and vision. That kind of motivation is called *intrinsic motivation*. The opposite, *extrinsic motivation*, is being motivated by others' approval, external rewards, or gifts. For simplicity's sake, I'll call them internal and external motivation.

The thing is, a little external motivation here and there doesn't hurt. I sometimes promise pizza parties to groups of students if they can significantly raise their class average. When I'm working with students individually, I sometimes promise to include them in my next presentation if they use the strategies and raise their grades. Remember my grandson who was failing math during the height of the pandemic? When he found out that his video game privileges would be restored if he raised his grades, he went from Cs and Ds to As and Bs in a couple of weeks.

Did you notice that framing? His parents emphasized that he *could* play games if he raised his grades, rather than emphasizing that he *couldn't* play games if his grades slipped. Encouragement, not threats. Yes, it's important to let your children know about the consequences they will face for their behavior. And it's important to carry out those consequences faithfully and matter-of-factly. But it's best to frame them as consequences, not punishment. And emphasize the positive consequences of good behavior. That way your child will learn: "If I engage in these behaviors, then I will see this result, but if I engage in those other behaviors, I will see that other result. It's up to me which result happens to me. It's in my hands." The parent worksheet at the end of the chapter gives you an opportunity to brainstorm what kinds of gifts and rewards might work for your child.

The Most Important External Motivator: Your Praise

Now I want to talk about how important praise is, especially for struggling students or students with a negative self-image. Regularly praising students can have a transformative effect on their motivation and on their relationship with the person giving them praise. But unskillful praise can actually hurt your child rather than help them, so let's talk about the most important aspects of skillful praise.

Skillful Praise Focuses on Process; Unskillful Praise Focuses on Results

Skillful praise focuses on process. That means that it requires you to pay enough attention to your child's process to be able to highlight the details of their choices. Paul L. Underwood, who wrote a *New York Times*[9] article intended to bring the findings from research on praise to a wider audience, suggested the following example. Praise your child *not* by saying, "I love it" or "Good job," but rather "Ooh, I see you chose to put the purple next to the brown—that's so interesting." But let's think about a more age-appropriate example for your high schooler. Let's say your child is working on a history project. You might say something like, "Oh, wow. On your poster about the year 1990, I see you chose to highlight both the end of apartheid in South Africa and the fall of the Berlin Wall. What an interesting contrast." This observation can convey interest and admiration without judgment.

Skillful Praise Focuses on Things Your Child Has Control Over; Unskillful Praise Focuses on Labels, or on You

Skillful praise also highlights things that your child has control over. For example, you might praise them for enjoying themselves, having fun, working hard, or being persistent. But praising them for "being a hard worker" or "being someone who never gives up" can have unintended consequences. That phrasing increases the chance that they will connect those characteristics to their self-worth. They could end up feeling that if they take a rest or thoughtfully decide to let go of a project, they will no longer be lovable. Phrasing such as "You're such a smart boy" or "You're such a pretty girl" also goes in this category. It gives your child a status that they can become afraid to lose. They can start to think, "Can something happen that will mean I'm not smart anymore?" We saw the effects of that thinking on Mrs. Valasco's students in the previous chapter.

Also watch out for giving feedback like, "I love it!" because it puts the focus on you. It might trigger the question, "Did I do something wrong if my parent doesn't love what I do?" Please don't get overly strict about these guidelines or be afraid to tell your child when you enjoy something that they do, but keep the underlying principle in mind.

Exception Alert! Some Children Should Be Praised for Being Smart

We learned in Chapter 7 that it is important to emphasize effort and not ability. That implies that we should always praise students for their efforts and never for how smart they are. For example, a parent might say, "Wow, you worked so hard on this project. Good job. Does it feel good to know you did your best?" Instead of: "Wow, this project shows what a genius you are." But it can be a little more complicated than that.

Some students, particularly minoritized students, often face the assumption that they are *not* smart. These students need to be praised for their efforts *and* for being smart. A parent might say to one of these students, "Wow, you worked so hard on this project. Great job. You are so smart and getting smarter every day with your efforts!" This feedback reflects a growth mindset but instills the idea in students that they are smart.

I have a colleague who teaches undergraduate biology and who starts every semester with a slide that reads, "Every student reading this slide is smart." She reports that every semester, young adults approach her after class with tears in their eyes because it's the first time anyone has ever told them they are smart. Tailor your praise to the personality and needs of your child in order to encourage a growth mindset and to challenge them to reach new heights.

Skillful Praise Is Regular and Creates Independence; Unskillful Praise Is Constant and Creates Dependency

This principle may seem counterintuitive, but in fact, too much praise can be a bad thing. Your child may start to feel like something is wrong if they're *not* being praised. The most important thing is to make sure your child feels seen and loved and that they know that what they do matters. As long as you are praising them enough to give them that sense, you don't need to do more.

Skillful Praise Is Genuine; Unskillful Praise is Inauthentic

You know how it's easy to tell when an actor is doing a bad job? Even when that actor is a trained professional making a lot of money? That's because human beings are wired to detect insincerity. Kids are *great* at it. Whether it's because praise is distracted and flat or over-the-top and excessive, kids will clock it. And when they do, it can demotivate them.[10]

An example of appropriate praise would be, "I really enjoyed your enthusiasm and detail when you taught me about the phases of the moon." Examples of less appropriate praise might be, "That phases of the moon thing was good," delivered in a flat, distracted tone with no eye contact or, "Woooowwww. That was amaaaaaazing!! I never would have expected that from you!"

OK, so now I've kind of backed you into a corner, right? Praise your child often *but not too much*. Do it *but don't do it wrong*. Next we'll talk about a principle that can get you out of this bind.

Skillful Praise is Descriptive Feedback Delivered with Curiosity

Instead of giving praise, think of giving your child *descriptive feedback*.[11] This avoids unintentionally turning your child's accomplishments into something done for your approval. Descriptive feedback is just noticing something your child is doing, describing some things about it, and then maybe asking a follow-up question.

Let's say your child is making a book of poetry. You would say, "Oh, I noticed you're writing poems and that some of them rhyme, but some of them don't. Can you tell me a little bit more about that?" If your child is working on a big lab report, you could say, "That lab report looks really involved. I noticed you have drawings on one page and a table of numbers on another page. Tell me more about it."

To give descriptive feedback:

1. Notice something your child is doing that is praiseworthy.

2. Describe something about what they are doing and note that you find it interesting, fascinating, cool, intriguing, compelling, striking, or other similar terms that convey interest without a value judgment.

3. Ask a follow-up question if it's appropriate.

Praise Roundup

Please know that imperfect praise is fine. I don't want you to feel so bogged down by all these guidelines that you can't say to your kid, "I love that drawing!" or "Great job doing so well on your history test today!" Both of those are much better than saying nothing. I'm sure you are doing a wonderful job as a parent, and I don't want you to start second-guessing yourself.

To recap this section:

- Skillful praise focuses on process and things your child has control over.

- Skillful praise is authentic, specific, and regular without being constant.

- Use *descriptive feedback* delivered with curiosity to strike the right balance.

  — Notice something your child is doing that is praiseworthy.

  — Describe something about what they are doing and note that you find it interesting, fascinating, cool, intriguing, compelling, striking, or other non-judgmental terms.

  — Ask a follow-up question if it's appropriate.

- For students who have been labeled "smart," praise their *efforts*.

- For students who have been labeled "not-smart," praise their efforts *and* affirm that they are smart.

Self-Esteem? Or Self-Compassion?[12]

How someone generally feels about themselves has an impact on whether they believe they can succeed. Our ultimate goal is to equip our children to move through the world with joy, confidence, and competence. Reaching this goal requires a balance between giving them positive and negative feedback. Nobody wants their children to be lazy, self-indulgent, or arrogant because they got too much positive feedback and too little negative feedback. And nobody wants their children to be underconfident, self-doubting, and depressed because they got too much negative feedback and too little positive feedback. I get it. We need to strike a balance, and each child may require different things to strike that balance. We can agree that we don't want our children to be self-indulgent, and we do want them to be self-confident. But what about self-esteem? Should we want our kids to have high self-esteem?

Self-esteem is how much a person approves of themselves. Of course we want our children to approve of themselves, but high self-esteem can also exist alongside low competence and overconfidence, as well as defensiveness in response to criticism and a tendency to blame others for unwanted situations.[13] Self-compassion is a more useful quality to focus on. Some people think that self-compassion sounds like letting ourselves off the hook. But, according to a University of California, Berkeley research article, self-compassion "involves treating ourselves with warmth and understanding in difficult times and recognizing that making mistakes is part of being human."[14] It has nothing to do with letting ourselves get away with stuff. In fact, it's just the opposite. Research shows that self-compassion helps us face up to our faults and improve them, while self-esteem can encourage us to ignore them because they don't match the way we think about ourselves.

These same researchers showed that people who demonstrated self-compassion, as opposed to self-esteem or silently repeating positive thoughts to distract themselves, worked harder to improve after failing a test. The advantage that self-compassion has over self-esteem is that you don't have to feel good about yourself to do it. The researchers note that "Self-compassion is associated with holding realistic self-appraisals." In other words, self-compassion makes room for the truth. Self-destruction tells lies in an overly negative direction: "I'm always so bad at everything. I'll never get better at this." Self-esteem can tell lies in an overly positive direction: "I'll just study for 20 minutes and ace this test because I'm so smart and awesome!" But self-compassion helps us see things as they are: "I'm having trouble with this concept now, but I can put in 45 minutes of Focused Study Session time tonight. Every time I've done that in the past, I've gained much more understanding and confidence. I can do this."

Self-compassion is about giving ourselves the sort of kindness and care that a skilled, loving parent would. So you are in a unique position to help your child develop self-compassion, both by modeling it yourself and by extending it to them. My worksheet on self-talk (Handout 8.5) also gives your child a concrete opportunity to develop these skills. The next chapter is also full of tools to help your child develop self-compassion and self-confidence. If the idea of self-compassion still sounds indulgent and soft to you, try to remember that it's just the opposite. Self-compassion makes us stronger because we are not relying on other people or inflated ideas of ourselves to give us validation and affirmation. We can give those things to ourselves.

Sometimes Motivation Isn't Enough: What to Do When Nothing Is Working

So far, we've looked at a range of tools you can use to help your child feel motivated to spend time on their schoolwork and learn subject matter deeply and securely. Now we're going to look at a few situations that might make these tools much less effective, or sometimes completely ineffective. I'll explain what you can do in each of these situations.

Refusal to Take Responsibility

If a student has a strong resistance to seeing how their behavior has contributed to a difficult situation and always defaults to blaming other people or outside circumstances, then it can be impossible to convince them to use learning strategies or any other support tools. If your child falls into this category, try not to meet their resistance head on or to convince them that they are wrong. Instead, listen to their account of why the responsibility lies outside themselves, empathize where you can, and then gently ask, "Looking back now, do you think there is anything you could have done so that the situation might have turned out differently?" If they say no, then ask, "If you were trying to help a friend in a similar situation, is there anything you might suggest to them, that they could do?" Sometimes people who resist taking responsibility are terrified that they are somehow doomed to fail. They don't want to try because they are convinced they're not going to succeed. When someone believes something very strongly, directly challenging their convictions often doesn't work. Instead, it's important to listen and gain their trust.

In addition to having your child complete Handout 8.6, try to regularly have gentle, patient conversations about how their behavior has contributed to particular outcomes, favorable and unfavorable. Acknowledge that there may be other people involved who also have some responsibility, but we choose to focus on our own behavior because we cannot control other people.

If your child does not respond to these interventions, consider working with a therapist or counselor you trust.

Overscheduled

If your child simply has too many things to do, then all of the learning strategies and motivational tools in the world might not improve their grades. Your child should have time for schoolwork, extracurricular activities like sports or music, and leisure time for things that they enjoy. I am definitely not suggesting that you should cut everything other than schoolwork out of your child's life so that they have time to focus on their homework. That is one of the most de-motivating things that can happen to a student. If you sense your child is overwhelmed, have a conversation with them about which activities they can let go of. If they don't want to let go of anything, gently explain that there just is not enough time for everything, and it will feel better and be more fun for them to do well in four things, say, instead of doing not-so-well in six things. You can also use a negotiating tactic here. Perhaps if two activities have to go, you can pick one and your child can pick the other. The important thing is not to make a one-sided decision. Your child should feel like they have input and understand why some changes to their schedule might be needed.

Skills Gap May Be Too Big

If a student is taking a typical sophomore chemistry class but has real trouble with fractions, decimals, and percentages, it might be difficult for them to do well. So if your child's performance does not respond to the learning strategies and you suspect they are lacking some foundational skills, ask their teacher to see whether your child has the basics to excel in the class. Sometimes, if there is a skills gap, a student may need to take extra classes during the summer. But sometimes it's enough to provide extra help with the missing skills during the school year. See what the teacher and the school are willing to provide. You can also investigate private tutoring options. See the tutor selection guide (Appendix C) for more information.

Another possibility to consider when your child has a skills gap is an undiagnosed learning disability. This is especially true if your child is very dedicated to their schoolwork but not getting the expected results, or if they seem uninterested in assignments involving reading or calculations. Listed in the Recommended Resources section are two informative websites to help you explore learning disabilities and their impact on learning. The website of the National Center for Learning Disabilities even offers a checklist tool to help parents recognize potential signs of learning disabilities or attention issues. Parents should also be aware that every state has different laws regarding learning disabilities, special education, 504 plans, and accommodations. Individualized Education Plans, or IEPs, are federal and apply nationwide. In general, it's important to know your federal, state, and local laws so that you can most effectively seek the accommodation your child may need.

Trauma

Traumatic life events happen to students all over the country every day, and trauma affects our ability to learn. Deaths in the family, bullying, and serious illness are just a few of the reasons that life might be too overwhelming for a student to focus on learning. It's reasonable to consider having your child take time off from school to address whatever they may be going through. If you know or suspect your child is dealing with trauma, I recommend seeking out a trusted mental health expert, school counselor, or qualified official to discuss your concerns and what course of action to take. These are suggestions, and final decisions about your child's health should always be undertaken in consultation with health professionals.

I once worked with a student named TJ who was diagnosed with brain tumors near the end of his sophomore year of high school and who underwent two major surgeries and chemotherapy over the next two years. After his first surgery, he couldn't walk, talk, eat, or drink. He ended up missing many, many weeks of school. But even though he took considerable time off in order to recover and rehabilitate himself, he was able to return to school and use learning strategies to graduate with a GPA higher than many students who did not have to deal with such challenging circumstances. Students can only overcome traumatic events when they get the care they need.

What Students Need in Order for Learning Strategies to Make a Difference

A student needs to know how to take responsibility for their actions; have enough time to work, rest, and play; possess an adequate academic foundation; not be in crisis; and have support for any learning disabilities. When those conditions are fulfilled, then metacognitive learning strategies can give a student everything they need to soar in school and enjoy themselves while doing it.

Defining *Core Content*

Students have a wide range of needs in terms of what keeps them motivated and positive. With the Handouts in chapters 8–11, I have tried to address as many of those needs as possible. But I also wanted to give you a way of making the most impact in the least amount of time. So I've selected resources that have a big impact on most students, grouped them together, and called them the *Core Content*. Every other resource in the book falls under the category *Additional Content*. Think of it this way: The Core Content is a toolbox that contains a hammer, wrench, and screwdriver—tools everyone needs. The Additional Content is a toolbox that contains a Phillips-head screwdriver, an Allen key, and an X-Acto knife, tools many people, but not everyone, needs. Your child may need a few handouts in the Additional Content, but maybe not all of it, whereas they probably *do* need all of the information in the Core Content.

What's in the *Core Content*

Everything in chapters 3–7 is in the Core Content. In chapters 8–11, selected resources are in the Core Content and the rest is Additional Content.

Is There Guidance About How to Use the Handouts in Chapters 8–11?

Since there are no scripts or script summaries in chapters 8–11, you may be wondering whether there is any guidance about how to use the materials in those chapters. At the end of each of those chapters, there's a bulleted list called a *handout roundup*. You can think of them like the script summaries of chapters 3–7. The handout roundups contain specific advice about how to use each handout during your sessions with your child, and they are for parents who prefer to have a step-by-step guide for using the materials.

In fact, the handout roundups serve a few important purposes:

1. If you return to the book later in the year, a subsequent year of your child's education, or even when another child enters high school, you can use the handout roundups to quickly review what each handout contains.

2. If you haven't been reading the handouts on the website, you can read a brief summary of the web-only handouts.

3. If you want step-by-step guidance about how to use the handouts during your sessions with your child, you'll find it in the handout roundups.

As you go through the roundup, I encourage you to read the bullet-pointed summary and then go straight to the handout and read it. Most of the handouts in chapters 8–11 are on the website, so if you read the roundup in the way that I suggest, you'll have a chance to practice accessing the handouts online. But if you're unable to visit the website while reading, everything that's essential to know is right there in the chapter.

A Worksheet Just for You

The very first worksheet in this chapter is the only worksheet in the book designed *just for you*. It was created to help you explore the information in the chapter and secure your understanding of it. I really hope you'll find it interesting and that it won't feel like work!

Handout Roundup for Chapter 8: Motivation Part 1: Getting Excited to Learn

- Handout 8.1 for Parents

  — This worksheet helps you reflect on some things you might do to boost your child's motivation, and it's also designed to help you figure out how well you have absorbed this chapter's content.

  — All answers to the content-based questions are found in the text you just read in chapter 8.

- Handout 8.2: My Interests and Things I Enjoy Doing

  — This worksheet asks your child to list their interests, hobbies, and some jobs they think they might be interested in doing.

  — If you are using this worksheet as part of your Core Content presentation of the chapter 8 materials, then first introduce the topic of motivation by sharing one or more of your own struggles with motivation that you wrote down in Handout 8.1.

  — This worksheet should take about 5 to 10 minutes.

- Handout 8.3: How Do You Prefer to Learn?

  — This worksheet asks your child lots of questions about how they like to learn. It explores preferences for study environment, study tools, and different ways of learning.

  — I recommend you go through Handout 8.3 with your child, unless they prefer privacy. You can read aloud the parts that I've written. Make mental notes about your child's preferences and keep the worksheet somewhere for reference.

  — This worksheet should take 10 to 15 minutes.

- Handout 8.4: How to Figure Out What You Are Actually Supposed to Be Doing

  — This handout is a step-by-step guide about how to go from total brain-fog-confusion to having a clear list of steps to follow in order to complete a task. It's included here in the book because it's so important.

  — Read Handout 8.4 to your child, and discuss it while doing so. Find out what they think about the suggestions, if any objections come up about following them. There are no right or wrong answers. Pushback is never a problem, and if your child has different or better ideas, those are welcome. There are questions at the end of the worksheet that your child should answer.

  — This worksheet should take 10 to 20 minutes, depending on how much discussion it generates.

- Handout 8.5: Self-Talk Journaling Worksheet

  — This worksheet teaches your child how to journal their self-talk. It encourages them to write down what they hear and then try writing a self-compassionate thought in response. The worksheet also contrasts self-compassion with a more aggressively positive self-talk, which is not as helpful because it creates direct conflict with negative self-talk.

  — Read the worksheet aloud and discuss it with your child. Perhaps try a couple of examples together. Consider being vulnerable and sharing some of your own self-talk.

  — This worksheet should take 5 to 15 minutes, depending on how much discussion it generates.

- Handout 8.6: Doing What *You* Can and Letting Go of the Rest

  — This worksheet teaches your child how to take responsibility for their actions. It gives the example of forgetting my umbrella in a rainstorm that appears in the chapter, as well as different accounts from students explaining why they thought they did well or badly on a test. Then the worksheet asks your child to list some recent disappointments, and for each, give three factors within their control and three factors outside of their control. For the factors within their control, they are asked to brainstorm what they could have done differently.

  — As you go through this worksheet with your child, you can read the parts that are in my voice and have your child read the statements from students. Again, discuss it as you read it together. Find out what they think. Remember, there are no right or wrong answers. When they get to the part to fill out, they can choose to do that with you or in private.

  — This worksheet should take 10 to 20 minutes, depending on how much discussion it generates.

Chapter 8 Handout Breakdown

All handouts are available on the website. The table in this breakdown shows all chapter 8 handouts, and **the handouts also reproduced in the book are shown in bold.**

NAME	TITLE
Handout 8.1	**Worksheet for Parents on Motivation**
Handout 8.2	Worksheet about My Interests and Things I Enjoy Doing
Handout 8.3	How Do You Prefer to Learn? (Worksheet)
Handout 8.4	**How to Figure Out What You Are Actually Supposed to Be Doing**
Handout 8.5	Self-Talk Journaling Worksheet
Handout 8.6	Doing What You Can and Letting Go of the Rest (Worksheet)

HANDOUT 8.1 **Worksheet for Parents on Motivation**

1. What are three questions that influence a person's motivation? _____
_____
_____
_____

2. Why do emotions influence learning? _____
_____
_____

3. Why aren't threats and fear good tools for motivating people? _____
_____
_____

4. What are three things I have trouble getting motivated to do? _____
_____
_____
_____

    (Circle the one(s) you would feel comfortable sharing with your child.)

5. What are three failures and difficulties I feel comfortable sharing with my child? _____
_____
_____
_____

6. Reflection question: How can I model for my child that it's okay to make mistakes and not have all the answers? _____
_____
_____
_____

7. What are some specific, concrete ways I can regularly monitor how my child is doing at school? _____
_____
_____
_____

8. If I think my parenting style is on the stricter side, what are three ways I can give my child more choices?

_____

_____

_____

9. If I think my parenting style is on the more permissive side, what are three ways I can give my child more structure and boundaries?_____

_____

_____

_____

10. What are three (or more) external rewards, like screen time or gifts, I might offer my child? _____

_____

_____

_____

11. How many times a day (or a week) do I praise my child? Do I think that it's enough? _____

_____

_____

_____

12. Is my child the type of student who needs to be praised only for effort or the type that needs to be praised for effort *and* for being smart? _____

_____

_____

13. List three attributes of skillful praise: _____

_____

_____

_____

14. List three attributes of unskillful praise: _____

_____

_____

_____

15. What are the three steps to offering descriptive feedback? _____

_____

_____

_____

16. What is the difference between self-esteem and self-compassion? _____

_____

_____

17. What are the benefits of self-compassion? _____

_____

_____

18. *(Complete after your child has done Handout 8.2.)* Here are three concrete ways I can demonstrate my interest in whatever my child is into: _____

_____

_____

_____

19. *(Complete after your child has done Handout 8.3.)* Even though I understand this could change at any time, right now my child seems to enjoy learning and studying in the following ways, with the following tools: _____

_____

_____

_____

Handouts 8.2–8.3 are only available on the website.

They are not crucial for understanding the book's content as you read it, but you will use them during your sessions with your child and may want to know what they contain. If so, go to www.studyandlearn.guide.

Handout 8.4 appears on the next page.

HANDOUT 8.4 How to Figure Out What You Are Actually Supposed to Be Doing

Have you ever looked at an assignment and thought, *"Wait, now what? What exactly am I actually supposed to be doing here? What does the teacher want from me?"* This is a universal experience. Adults go through the same thing at their jobs sometimes, wondering what a boss or a client expects of them. Fortunately, there are concrete steps you can take to figure out the answers you need.

STEP 1:

Gather all of the materials that tell you what the assignment is supposed to be. This may include your class syllabus, the document the teacher may have given you at the very beginning of the year that lays out the class plan for the whole year. There may also be specific handouts or online documents for that assignment, as well as class notes you took while the teacher was explaining it. Gather all of that material and read it carefully. It might help to make brief notes about the important points, for example, "Chapters 8–12, 1,000 words, different rulers during Ming dynasty, due 4/12."

STEP 2:

If you are still confused about what you should be doing, and there is still time, **respectfully ask your teacher for clarification**. Begin by sharing what you *have* figured out and ask about the specific things you are confused about. For example, "Ms. Jones, I get that we're supposed to write 1,000 words on how different emperors ruled during the Ming dynasty, but I don't understand how many emperors we have to write about."

To really impress your teacher, come up with possible answers to your questions and ask if it's okay for you to do that. For example, if you only want to write about two emperors, you could ask, "Ms. Jones, I get that we're supposed to write 1,000 words on how different emperors ruled during the Ming dynasty, but I just wanted to ask you—is it okay if I only write about Hongwu and Jiajing?" Not only do you make your teacher's job easier and demonstrate that you have invested time and thoughtfulness into the assignment, but you also get another opportunity to ask for what you want.

STEP 3:

If there isn't enough time to ask your teacher, then contact a friend who is likely to know the answer. You shouldn't have to do this more than once or twice because in the future, you will begin your assignments early enough to be able to ask the teacher if you need to. You will also begin to notice when you need clarification, even as the assignment is first being given.

STEP 4:

Now that you know what you should be doing, **break the task down into smaller steps**. For a term paper, your breakdown might look like this:

Term Paper Breakdown

1. Brainstorm and think about a main idea

2. Gather primary and secondary sources

3. Do active reading and make notes

4. Outline

5. Write first draft

6. Revise

Sometimes you'll realize that a step in your breakdown needs to be broken down even further when you get to it. For example, the breakdown of Step 3, "Do active reading and make notes," might be:

Step 3 Breakdown

1. Chapter 8 from textbook

2. *Letters to a Young Poet* by Rainer Maria Rilke

3. *A Ringing Glass: A Biography of Rainer Maria Rilke* by Donald Prater

4. Class notes

As you can see, each of those steps can be broken down even further. Break a task down into the smallest steps that you need in order to feel like you can tackle them successfully. Whenever my daughter, the one with the PhD, feels stuck about anything, she breaks it down. She gave me permission to share one with you. This was for a day when she was feeling particularly unsure of herself.

Overwhelm Breakdown

1. Get out of bed

2. Arrange pencils on desk

3. Open laptop and file

4. Take a deep breath

5. Break down beginning of task

The point here is that you never have to feel bad about feeling stuck or not knowing what to do. You can always break something down into steps that feel manageable for you, and if you feel like you've exhausted all your options, you can always ask for help.

Motivation Part 2: Dealing with Failure

We learned in the last chapter that knowing it's okay to make mistakes helps us feel supported in working toward our goals. In fact, how we feel about obstacles in general—mistakes, failures, or any other kind of negative feedback—has a decisive effect on our motivation and therefore on our ability to reach our goals. Put simply, it's just plain harder to believe that we can succeed when we're facing failure, negativity, and resistance. When we lose faith in ourselves, it's more difficult to put forth the effort to get what we want.

I decided to devote a whole chapter to failure because how we handle it can mean the difference between barely surviving and exuberantly thriving. Fortunately, dealing skillfully with failure is something that everyone can get better at by practicing specific strategies.

Students Will Do as You Do, Not as You Say

The previous chapter laid out a range of things that both you and your child can *do* in order to boost motivation. This chapter is more about encouraging your child to have a healthy *attitude* about failure. Although I do recommend some actions you can take—like giving feedback in a helpful way, sharing a failure or two with your child, and expressly telling them that you respect how they define success—most of the suggestions are either about what *not* to do or about having a helpful attitude. The thing is, you can't really tell your child to have a particular attitude. If that were possible, we would all be walking around carefree, happy, and entirely unbothered by what anyone else might say about us. Instead, attitudes must be modeled.

In this chapter, I explain how you can model a healthy attitude about failure for your child by using eight distinct messages. I've included worksheets and handouts that prompt your child to do a lot of thinking about mistakes, risk, failure, and success. Our goal here is for your child to see failure as *fuel* for growth and development. Over time, we want them to begin to automatically see obstacles as *valuable opportunities for learning*.

General Recommendation: Avoid Sarcasm

I enjoy irony and satire as much as the next person, but over the years I have found that sarcasm has an element of meanness that does not help students get into the best frame of mind to learn. It tends to promote fear and shame instead. I raised two daughters, so I know that you will be on the *receiving* end of no small amount of sarcasm from your tweens and teens. But try your best not to give it back, particularly when your child is trying to learn something or do schoolwork. You may wonder why I've included this recommendation in a chapter about failure and negative feedback. The answer is that sarcasm is essentially a form of negative feedback. It basically says, "Why are you wasting my time with your stupidity?" And although it's 100% human to feel that way, I don't believe it's a message we want to be sending to our children. *How* we say something is sometimes even more important than *what* we say.

Now on to our eight healthy messages.

Make-Friends-With-Failure Message #1: It's Perfectly Okay to Fail

You may worry that if your child doesn't have a fear of failure, then they'll happily come home with Ds and Fs. But children want to do well. It's just that when they believe they *can't* fulfill someone else's expectations, sometimes their rebellious side comes out to defend the vulnerable part of them that is afraid of failing and losing someone else's love and approval. The rebellious side comes to the rescue and says, "Don't worry about their stupid expectations. *I'll* love you even *more* if you tank that test." That rebellious part is the part that pretends not to care about doing well, or that might even be gleeful about defying expectations and getting bad grades. But if we tell our children that it's okay to fail and that mistakes are normal, it lets them know that there's no *need* to rebel. It lowers the hurdle for them to meet our expectations, and it gives them the support they need to do their best.

Make-Friends-With-Failure Message #2: Everyone Fails, and Everyone Has Tough Feelings about It

I think it's a great idea to share one or two of your own failures with your child in order to let them know that feeling bad about failure is a universal human experience. I'm not suggesting you treat your child like a therapist or express a lot of painful, complicated feelings that they won't know what to do with. Choose a failure that either led to something even better happening in your life or one where the heartbreak has already faded. The idea is to let your child know that failure does hurt, and it's okay to hurt when it happens. Many people try to pretend that failure doesn't hurt, and that's a mistake. Suppressing strong feelings may make things easier in the short term, but—as you may have heard from all the pretend therapists on TV—if we don't release our feelings in healthy ways, they can end up wreaking havoc on our lives.

Pretending that failure doesn't hurt at all might help us to keep going in the short term. But before too long we'll have to give up on our goal because the pain or frustration of encountering normal obstacles is going to eventually be too big to exist alongside our insistence that failure doesn't affect us. We will end up limiting our possibilities because we refuse to feel some temporary pain. But if it's *okay* to admit that failure hurts, then that hurt becomes much less of a big deal and it doesn't have to stop us from going after our goal. Many actors, singers, and dancers give themselves an entire 24 hours to be depressed after a bad audition or a rejection. Accepting that failure hurts and knowing that it's perfectly human to hurt is the first step to moving on. Being honest about our emotions and fully feeling them helps us to leave them in the past. When students know that there's nothing *wrong* with failure, then they can bounce back from it more easily because they won't be clobbered with shame when they're hit with tough but temporary feelings.

Make-Friends-With-Failure Message #3: There Are No Stupid Questions

Regularly remind your child that no question is stupid or too basic for them to ask. Feel free to encourage them—in a kind and curious tone—to figure out the answers themselves but do your best never to shame your child for asking a sincere question.

Make-Friends-With-Failure Message #4: You're Getting This Critical Feedback Because You Are Cared For

Remember those researchers who discovered that letting students know the *purpose* of critical feedback got more students to use it to their benefit (see pages 73–74)? You can do the same thing. Just explain to your child that the purpose of your feedback is to ultimately make their lives easier and more enjoyable. So, every time you ask your child to make a change to their behavior, let them know *why*, and ground that reason in their own happiness and well-being. When you do that, they can receive your feedback not as judgmental criticism but instead as support and belief in themselves. You might say something like, "I want you to do the dishes, so that it becomes automatic and you can be a good housemate in a few years when you leave home." The more often you can use this way of giving your child feedback, the more they will learn to hear your requests and suggestions as loving kindness instead of an indication that something is wrong with them.

Make-Friends-With-Failure Message #5: When Feedback Is Brutal, It's All Right to Cry

Of course, sometimes feedback won't be given kindly. But you can help your child have the sweetest revenge by helping them realize that they can use that feedback to get better. You may not want to use that language but find a way to split the difference between (a) teaching your child to use the *energy* of their hurt and anger to move forward and (b) helping them understand that the person who gave the feedback may have had good intentions, and therefore your child can feel free to let go of any hurt and anger they may have toward that person.

If your child reacts to negative feedback with difficult emotions, that's actually a golden opportunity for them to learn that not only can they *survive* feedback that lands in a hurtful way, but they can even *use* that criticism to their advantage, whether or not it was meant constructively.

I'd like to explain why acknowledging the pain caused by negative feedback is more helpful than trying to push it away. Feelings generally arise instantaneously. Most of the time, we don't choose them. They just show up. We certainly choose how to *respond* to them, but the feelings themselves generally arrive unasked for. For example, we can feel a big wave of anger and choose to take deep breaths, talk with a trusted friend, journal, or do some physical exercise instead of saying hurtful words or engaging in physical violence. Or we could feel a big wave of love for someone but still refrain from hugging them because we want to respect their boundaries. Sure, we could suppress those feelings so that we don't feel them, but then they can go underground to wreak havoc on us in other ways, usually by coming out at inappropriate times to hurt ourselves or others. But *acknowledging* and *releasing* feelings means that we can move on from them.

The great thing about this approach is that it will work whether your child is naturally tough or sensitive. If they are a tough cookie and only the most brutal feedback bothers them, then whenever they do encounter a disappointment that knocks them for a loop, it's natural for them to think, "Oh, this isn't a feeling I'm used to. This probably means I'm not meant to be doing something that makes me feel so bad." But learning to acknowledge hurtful feelings and use the feedback to grow will teach your Teflon kid that not even painful feelings can stop them. If your child is the type to be devastated for days by an unkind facial expression, then it will be a huge help for them to know that those feelings aren't bad or wrong, and that they don't need to try to stop having the feelings in order to make progress and grow. Your delicate child will learn from this approach that they can be sensitive *and* unstoppable.

Make-Friends-With-Failure Message #6: It Might Not Be as Bad as You Think; Negative Feedback Can Be Easy to Address

I submitted a journal article recently. When it came back from the peer reviewers covered in corrections, along with a request to revise and resubmit it, my heart sank. I quickly forwarded it to my daughter, closed down the file, and let it disappear into the depths of my inbox. A few days later when we were on the phone for other reasons, she asked brightly, "So, what did you think of the reviewers' comments?"

"Ugh. Don't even remind me! I haven't looked at it yet. How bad is it?"

"Oh! I didn't think it was bad at all. I thought it was really encouraging and that all the changes they asked for were really doable."

After hearing her say that, I was able to look at the article, and I saw that she was right! But if I had remembered message #6, that it might not be as bad as I thought, I might have been able to look at it without her encouragement. The tragic thing is that if I hadn't spoken to her, I may well have decided not to resubmit at all.

I actually had a similar experience with the first textbook study guide that I ever wrote, except back then, my daughter was an infant, and publishers still did everything on paper. I got the draft back, and there were a ton of red pen markings on every single page. I felt so overwhelmed that I immediately put it back in the envelope. Three weeks later, when I only had one more week before my deadline to re-submit, I finally forced myself to look at the pages. Guess what? All of the suggestions were really easy to implement. I had tortured myself for nothing.

That's why I want your child to use Handout 9.5 when they get feedback that feels devastating, so that they don't have to torture themselves like I did. It's a step-by-step process that leads students through dealing with difficult feedback. First, they take the time to get their emotions out and remind themselves of failures that people they admire have experienced. Next, they make themselves physically comfortable and review the feedback, taking notes in a specific format and writing down questions about everything they don't understand. Then they reward themselves for facing the feedback. After that, it's time to get their questions answered. Finally, they reflect on the whole process and see whether they believe that facing the difficult feedback led to a better outcome than rejecting it.

Make-Friends-With-Failure Message #7: Flip the Script—Embrace Mistakes as Opportunities Instead of Regretting Them

Nelson Mandela said, "I never lose. I either win or I learn." In other words, whenever you go for a particular goal or result, there are only two outcomes. You either get the result you wanted, or you get some feedback that tells you how to move forward toward that result or toward another goal. According to Mandela, losing is just an incorrect label for *learning*. In that spirit, we want to consistently communicate to our children that mistakes are opportunities for learning. We want to model for them that we can respond to making a mistake by thinking, "Ah! Great! Another learning opportunity!" If we combine message #7 and message #5, we can see that expressing and releasing our initial disappointment *makes room for* recognizing that we have an opportunity. Most of the time, making a mistake isn't *wrong*. All of the time, it's a chance to grow.

Make-Friends-With-Failure Message #8: I Respect Your Definition of Success

So, one way to define failure is that it is the absence of success.

Let's say you and I are both in our kitchens, trying to make pralines. The sugar-milk-butter mixture has to reach just the right temperature in order to harden into crunchy pralines. If it doesn't, then it will turn out more like chewy pralines. I pride myself on my pralines. If they don't harden properly, I consider that a failure. If I made a chewy batch of candy, sure, I could choose to look at the bright side—that people might still enjoy it—but in order to reach *my* goal, I would need to make another batch. But maybe you love crunchy *and* chewy pralines.

For you, a batch of candy "gone wrong" would not be a failure at all! In other words, for me, success means crunchy pralines. For you, success means crunchy *or* chewy pralines.

Why are we talking about sugary Southern treats? Because I want you to know that it's important to understand what success means to your child in order to be able to support them appropriately through their failures. Ambitious, hard-driving parents with more relaxed, easygoing children may consider their children's successes to be failures, which can be hard on those children. Relaxed, easygoing parents with ambitious, hard-driving children may not understand what the big deal is about getting a B+. Both kinds of parents need to take the time to understand what success means to their children and respect those definitions.

In Handout 9.6 I ask your child for their definition of success. I encourage you to have a conversation with your child about their answers. If your child's idea of success is different from your idea of success for them but doesn't seem unethical, amoral, or self-destructive to you, see how it feels to validate and encourage their idea. But if you just can't get on board with it, then see if you can work out a compromise during that conversation that works for both of you.

Asking you to use a helpful definition of success is really just another way of asking you to set clear expectations. If your child knows that you will celebrate a B in a class they've really been struggling with, it might give them the confidence to go for the A. Then again, if you have a child who needs to be pushed, and they're within reach of the A, communicate that to them in a loving, supportive way. If you take the time to revise your expectations—and what counts as success—according to your child's best efforts on a particular day, then you will be giving them the best chance to feel like a winner.

No Tiptoeing

During these two chapters about motivation, I have encouraged you to be generous with your empathy and praise. But I want to be clear that I'm not asking you to walk on eggshells around your child, afraid you're going to break or ruin them. And I'm certainly not suggesting that you be dishonest with them. Kids are excellent at picking up on that kind of fear or deception, and they respond to it by wondering what's wrong with *them*. Instead, be yourself while you balance high expectations with fierce compassion and consistent praise. The more you skillfully praise your child, and the more empathy and kindness you show them, the more latitude you're going to have when it's time to get tough with them.

Finally, leave the ultimate responsibility for your child's performance with your child. Simply let them know you will be there if they need a hand or a shoulder to cry on.

Handout Roundup for Chapter 9

Motivation Part 2: Dealing with Failure

Information about the handout roundups can be found in chapter 8 (page 101).

- Handout 9.1: Quick Reference List of Helpful Practices and Attitudes About Failure for Parents

  — This summary of helpful attitudes and actions to take with your child regarding failure was created to be a convenient resource for you.

- Handout 9.2: Dealing with Setbacks, Mistakes, and Failure

  — This handout introduces the idea that mistakes and failure can be advantageous and lead to growth by quoting other students' ideas about mistakes. It also reveals that students who did better on an international math assessment felt comfortable making mistakes, while students who did worse were embarrassed about their mistakes.

  — Give it to your child and have them read it aloud. Engage in a short discussion once they have finished.

  — This worksheet should take about 5 minutes or less.

- Handout 9.3: Stumbling Blocks or Stepping Stones

  — This handout tells the story of Sydnie, a student who was in tears about getting Ds on her first two tests in college, but who went on to make a 4.0 that same semester. Additional stories are told of a band who overcame a terrible dress rehearsal to give a triumphant performance and a basketball team who overcame a two-game deficit to win a championship. Take-home messages: You have the power to turn a stumbling block into a stepping stone. What's *in* the way *is* the way.

  — Have your child read some or all of this handout aloud if they need extra encouragement about bouncing back from a failure. Briefly discuss the two take-home messages. Ask them if they can think of a time when they turned a stumbling block into a stepping stone.

  — This handout should take about 5 minutes.

- Handout 9.4: Mistakes and Failure Worksheet

  — This worksheet is an extensive one that probes your child's attitudes about and understanding of mistakes and failure.

  — You will use this worksheet to explicitly share some of the content in Chapter 9, specifically from the sections *Everyone Fails* (#2), *No Stupid Questions* (#3),

When Feedback Is Brutal (#5)*, and Flip the Script* (#7)*.* You can also use it as an opportunity to share one or more of your own failures from the parent worksheet on motivation.

— I recommend that you talk through the worksheet out loud, with opportunity for discussion and clarification. You have an answer key, but listen carefully to your child's answers because they might well be more insightful than mine. Use this worksheet to have a lively discussion about all of the principles in this chapter.

— This worksheet should take 10 to 20 minutes, depending on how much discussion it prompts.

■ Answer Key 9.4A: Answer Key to Handout 9.4

■ 9.5 Handout: A Process for Dealing with Negative Feedback or Failure

— This handout is a step-by-step guide to dealing with major, devastating failures or negative feedback. It is described at length in the chapter.

— Depending on your child, have them read it aloud, read it out loud to them, or let them quietly read it alone. Discuss it together or make it clear to them that you are available to talk about it or to answer any questions they may have.

— This worksheet should take 10 to 15 minutes to discuss. You may also choose to take a minute to simply introduce it as an available resource.

■ Handout 9.6: Worksheet—Defining Success

— This worksheet lays out some different definitions of success and asks your child to give theirs. It is intended to help you follow my recommendation to respect your child's definition of success.

— Have your child read the handout aloud and then either answer the questions aloud or privately before sharing their answers with you. Have a discussion about it, and reassure them that you understand and respect their definition of success.

— This worksheet should take 5 to 10 minutes.

Chapter 9 Handout Breakdown

All handouts except the answer keys are available on the website. The table in this breakdown shows all chapter 9 handouts, and **the handouts also reproduced in the book are shown in bold.**

NAME	TITLE
Handout 9.1	**Quick Reference List of Helpful Practices and Attitudes about Failure for Parents**
Handout 9.2	Dealing with Setbacks, Mistakes, and Failure
Handout 9.3	Stumbling Blocks or Stepping Stones
Handout 9.4	Mistakes and Failure Worksheet
Answer Key 9.4A	**Answer Key for Mistakes and Failure Worksheet**
Handout 9.5	A Process for Dealing with Negative Feedback or Failure
Handout 9.6	Worksheet—Defining Success

HANDOUT 9.1	Quick List of Helpful Practices and Attitudes about Failure for Parents

- Avoid sarcasm.

- Regularly remind your child that there are no stupid questions.

- When you give critical feedback, also express you believe your child can rise to meet it and say which aspect of life you are trying to help them enjoy.

- Give space for emotions. Remind your child that Handout 9.5, A Process for Dealing with Failure, can be used to get their feelings out.

- Treat the possibility of your child's failure neutrally. Don't be unresponsive or invalidate their strong emotions, but don't get drawn into a story that their lives will be ruined by this one failure.

- Embrace mistakes, failure, and negative feedback as opportunities for growth.

- Respect your child's definition of success, be aware of your own, and expect both to change.

- Skillfully praise your child for how they deal with tough feedback.

- Leave ultimate responsibility for your child's performance with them.

Handouts 9.2–9.4 are only available on the website.

They are not crucial for understanding the book's content as you read it, but you will use them during your sessions with your child and may want to know what they contain. If so, go to www.studyandlearn.guide.

Answer Key 9.4A appears on the next page.

Answer Key for Mistakes and Failure Worksheet

These are just some possible answers to these questions. There are no wrong answers. Listen carefully to your child's thoughts, feelings, and insights. You can offer the answers here as alternatives, but never as the "right" answer. Questions that are only a matter of opinion or ask about a person's past experience are left blank. Therefore, answers appear only for select questions.

Making Mistakes and Failing

1. Is it shameful to make a mistake or to fail? Why or why not?

2. Do you think there has ever been a person who never experienced failure or the difficult feelings that come with it? Why or why not?

3. Is it possible for two people to look at the same outcome and for one of them to interpret it as a success and the other to interpret it as a failure? Can you think of an example? Why do you think this happens?

4. What are some advantages of making a mistake?

    You can learn from your mistakes. You have a better chance of not making that mistake again.

5. What are some disadvantages of being afraid to make mistakes?

    You miss out on learning; you don't find out that you may have wrong ideas about things or not understand them completely.

6. Can there be an advantage to making a *lot* of mistakes?

    If you make a lot of mistakes, it means that you're probably trying a lot. Many basketball players who make the most shots also miss the most shots because they *take* the most shots.

7. What do you think would happen to someone who did not experience a significant failure until they were 18 years old?

    They would have no skills for bouncing back, and so they could be completely wiped out when they finally face a failure. It could have a devastating effect on them.

8. What opportunities do your teachers give you to make mistakes *before* you take a test? **Homework, in-class problems, quizzes.**

9. Is failure necessarily bad? Explain what Nelson Mandela meant when he said, "I either win or I learn."

Failure and Emotions

1. Is it better to try not to care about failure or to acknowledge that it hurts?

2. What happens when we try to pretend that failure doesn't hurt?

   We may avoid similar situations in the future, costing ourselves opportunities for learning, growth, and joy.

3. If we have an experience of failure but suppress our emotions about it, what might happen the next time we find ourselves in a similar situation?

   All the feelings could come up again, and it could feel even worse and harder to deal with.

The Courage to Make Mistakes, Especially in Public

1. Why does the idea of being wrong in public feel so scary to most people?

   Human beings have a natural fear of people thinking bad things about them. It feels scary to think that people might believe we are stupid.

2. What are some advantages of being willing to make a mistake or be wrong in front of other people?

   We find out that they don't automatically conclude that we are stupid or stop being our friend. We correct our mistakes. We learn.

3. What can you do if you ask an honest question and someone calls it stupid?

   Know that it's their problem, not mine. Leave their attempt to shame me over there with them.

4. If you wanted to try to figure out the answer to a question before asking someone, how could you do that?

   Try to think it out, internet search, look it up in a book.

5. What could happen if you didn't ask a question because you were afraid of being made fun of?

   I wouldn't find out the answer and I could lose points on an assignment, quiz, or test. Worse, I would miss out on learning that information, which could be useful in all sorts of ways in the future.

6. What's the worst thing that could happen to someone if they asked a question and someone else made fun of them?

   They might feel embarrassed for a few minutes, hours, or maybe even days, but that feeling will pass.

7. What is the *best* thing that could happen if you started asking more questions?

   I could learn a lot more things and do better and have more fun with my schoolwork. I could figure out how to do the thing I want to do most in life.

Setting Up: Time Management, Work Space, and Brain Health

Up to this point, we've covered *what* your child should be doing and *how* and *why* they should be doing it. In this chapter, we'll look at *when* and *where* your child will be studying and learning. In the final part of the chapter, you'll learn how to help keep your child's brain in tip-top condition.

We're going to talk about four things in this chapter:

- Time management—schedules, calendars, when to start homework

- Handling distractions—saying no, digital detoxing

- Choosing a work space that fits

- Keeping the brain in shape—nutrition, movement, and sleep

Time Management and Scheduling

Here are the principles of time management you'll communicate to your child with this chapter's material:

1. Schedule in order of priority. (Handout 10.3)

2. Use the syllabus to fill out your calendars. (Handout 10.4)

3. Fill out a term calendar. (Handout 10.4)

4. Fill out a weekly calendar every week. (Handout 10.5)

5. Start your homework as soon as it is given.

6. Learn to say no and set boundaries to protect your time. (Handout 10.7)

Nuts and Bolts of Scheduling: Start Big and End Small

The following exercise introduces the idea of calendars and scheduling to your child.

Ask your child to imagine that they have a big bucket and that there are four things that need to fit into the bucket: water, some pebbles, a few very large rocks, and sand. Then ask them what *order* they would put those things into the bucket, to ensure that everything fits. The expected answer is: large rocks, pebbles, sand, water. The idea here is that if you want everything to fit, you have to make sure the big things go in before the small things. And that's the principle that guides effective scheduling. The big rocks represent bigger projects and exams, as well as large time commitments like classes, work shifts, and important events and meetings. The pebbles represent minor quizzes and daily homework assignments. The sand represents more flexible activities like social time or meals. The water is everything else that has to get done during the course of a day but which can be moved around other things. This includes unscheduled free time for fun stuff.

Make the point that if you decide to put the water or sand in first, there won't be any room left for the big rocks. You might even share with your child that spending time distracted on social media means that sometimes *you*, as an adult, don't even get to some of your big rocks. You can also point out that after the rocks are in the bucket, there are all these little pockets for the sand and water to go. Those pockets represent ten minutes here or five minutes there when it might be possible to complete a small task or part of a larger task. Sometimes we need to use our breaks to rest, but sometimes we can use them to be productive.

Handout 10.3 gives your child an opportunity to express these ideas in their own words immediately after you do this exercise with them.

The Syllabus as the Starting Point for Scheduling

Managing our time begins with figuring out exactly what we have to do. For a student, that process often begins with the *class syllabus*, or the master plan that lays out the dates of homework assignments, projects, quizzes, and tests. Handout 10.4 teaches your child how to read a syllabus and get the information they need in order to fill out their calendars. They will eventually use all of their class syllabi to complete their calendars.

What if none of your child's teachers uses a syllabus? In that case, your child can use materials given to them in class, their notes, and any online class calendars or scheduling information to fill in their calendars. As soon as new dates are posted or announced, your child can add them to their calendar. Handout 10.4 also addresses what to do when there is no syllabus.

Term Calendar

In order to start putting big rocks in the bucket, your child needs a calendar that shows the entire term. Sometimes a calendar like this is called *Term-at-a-Glance*, and I give you a few ways of creating one in Handout 10.4. The purpose of a term calendar is to give your child the big picture so they're not just operating on a day-to-day basis, constantly being caught off guard by upcoming deadlines. Your child will use their class syllabi or other sources of scheduling information to enter into the term calendar all major projects, tests, quizzes, papers, trips, and events like games, performances, or school dances, as well as any important social events they are expected to attend, like birthdays or anniversaries.

Weekly Calendar

Now that most of the big rocks are in the bucket, it's time to handle the smaller items. A weekly calendar is an excellent tool for day-to-day time management. Handout 10.5 gives you a template, plus some additional suggestions for getting a weekly calendar. This calendar should include anything that appears on that particular week of the term calendar plus all after-school activities (clubs, teams, lessons, rehearsals, practices), study time, social time, and sleep.

The amount of time your child needs to spend studying and doing homework will vary widely. Some students may be able to complete their assignments in a relatively short amount of time while others may find themselves frequently burning the midnight oil. Crucial questions to consider are whether the homework culture at your child's school is a good fit for them and whether they may be experiencing burnout. Pay attention to the number of hours your child is regularly spending on schoolwork and *how* they're spending that time. Ideally, they'll be using learning strategies in an appropriate study environment to make their learning efforts efficient and supportive of their ultimate goals.

Start Homework as Soon as It Is Given

Here's an important principle for your child to keep in mind as they decide how to divide up their time: start each homework assignment as soon as it is given, not just before it's due. This way, they give themselves time to use the learning strategies during an adequate number of Focused Study Sessions. If they finish earlier than expected, they can use that time to catch up on some other things that might be taking longer than expected. Or they can just relax or do something they enjoy. If your child gets in the habit of beginning homework as soon as it is assigned, they will learn not to put things off in general. A life without procrastination sounds pretty good, right? It can start with this principle.

But your child may find life unbearably boring unless they're somehow living on the edge and need the pressure of deadlines to get in gear. Lots of perfectly happy, successful people (including yours truly) live that way. You can still encourage them to start their assignments as soon as they are given. Even if they can reduce their habit of starting things at the last minute by a tiny bit, those efforts will have meaningful benefits.

Eliminating Distractions

In this section, we'll look at how to minimize major distractions, which usually come in the form of social activity, both online and in real life.

Saying No and Setting Boundaries

Learning to say no is a big part of time management. It has become popular in recent years to depict the act of saying yes as a way of keeping ourselves open to growth and possibility. But within every yes is a no. And within every no is a yes. For example, if I say yes to a lunch date,

I'm saying no to all of the other things I could be doing during that time. If I say no to that same appointment, I'm saying yes to another activity I might enjoy more and find more fulfilling. Ideally, every person spends their time having as much fun and doing as much good as possible. But the demands on our time and attention are endless. So, in order to say yes to maximum fun and maximum usefulness, we have to learn to say no. I've included what I hope is an entertaining worksheet at the end of this chapter—Handout 10.7—to try to communicate to your child the importance of asking for what they want, courageously facing conflict, and finding compromises.

Notifications Off: Digital Detoxing

Now I want to talk about the number one distraction in almost all of our lives: notifications and content from various social media platforms and apps on our phones, tablets, and computers. How we manage these devices makes such a huge impact on our time management that I wanted to devote a whole section to the topic.

I encourage you to get your child's permission to disable sound and banner notifications for all of the apps on their computer, tablet, and/or phone, especially the social media and messaging apps. Just disabling sounds and notification vibrations on their phone could be enough as long as they keep their phone in a separate room or area while they study. Your goal here is to minimize distractions while they are trying to learn. Another good option might be to just put their phone in airplane mode whenever they are studying.

I've also included an App Detox Worksheet inspired by my grandson. One of the ways that he turned his grades around and got his gaming privileges back was by uninstalling all of his social media apps on his phone. His phone automatically tracked how much time he spent on each app, so he knew which ones were the biggest time wasters. Once he had gotten his grades back up, he added the apps back one by one, in order of least to most usage. If he found his grades were slipping, then he removed the most recently re-installed app until he got his grades up again. Through that process, he was eventually able to maintain his GPA while having all of his phone apps installed. When he realized how much more rewarding it was to do well in school than waste time on the apps, it broke his addiction for good. So he could use Snapchat, for example, without getting obsessed with it.

If you want to explore this topic even further, do a search for "digital detox apps" and you'll find a lot of options, including free ones. Depending on the phone your child has, there may also be utilities or built-in apps that track screen time or have a digital detox function. Consider checking the options you have on all of your devices too. You might be surprised how much productivity both you and your child can recover by taking control of your devices and realizing how they constantly vie for our attention. There's a reason Silicon Valley bigwigs keep their own children away from most of the technology they create. I've included a section in Handout 10.1 that asks your child to list all of their devices and how they plan to keep themselves distraction-free during their Focused Study Sessions.

It's a Lifelong Learning Process

Finally, explain to your child that time management is a lifelong process. How we spend our time directly reflects our desires and priorities, and those change throughout our lives.

There's no problem making mistakes and thinking, for example, "Oh, I wish I had studied longer for my test instead of going to that party." Or the other way around. We learn from our time-management mistakes and learn to do better in the future.

You may consider discussing your own time-management challenges with your children, so that they get the feeling that you're all in this together. The whole family could even sit down on Sunday evenings to fill out their weekly calendars together.

The Room Where It Happens: Your Child's Work Space

Now let's talk about the physical environment in which your child will learn and study. Ideally, it will be comfortable enough to promote relaxed concentration and structured enough to signal that it's work time. This balance will be different for different people. One kid might do best curled up in a ball on a couch surrounded by pillows, while another might do best on a rigid chair sitting in front of a nearly empty desk where everything is arranged at perfect right angles. We often find out what works best for us through trial and error, so you might want to encourage your child to experiment with different options.

The next thing to consider is how loud or quiet a work space is. Some students prefer complete silence. Others can only concentrate if there is background noise or music. For others, it depends on the subject. Kids who need quiet might want ear plugs or noise-canceling ear buds or headphones. Kids who need some background sounds, or who live in lively households, might find a white-noise machine helpful. And for kids who prefer to listen to music while they work, you could suggest they try listening to instrumental music. They might find it easier to concentrate without hearing lyrics. Finally, you want to make sure the volume isn't turned up too high. Once our hearing cells die, they don't regenerate.

Lighting is a third important factor, after furniture and the sound environment. Again, preferences here are highly individual. Does your child like dimmer or brighter light, or have a sensitivity to fluorescent or LED lighting? Do they need a desk lamp? Are they sensitive to the color of the walls or wallpaper?

Finally, your child's work space should be large enough for the materials and tools they're working with.

Handout 10.1, a worksheet about study preferences, invites your child to express all of their preferences, but I am in no way suggesting that we can't function unless we have everything exactly the way we want. It's just that paying too little attention to our own comfort means we might burn ourselves out earlier than necessary. The idea is to give ourselves what we prefer whenever we can, so that when things *don't* go our way, we have enough reserve in the tank to rise above it. "Whatever doesn't kill you makes you stronger," goes the popular saying. But sometimes whatever doesn't kill you just makes it easier for the next thing to take you out of commission.

Work Space Options

Let's take a look at *where* we can find potential work spaces, either inside or outside the home.

A student's bedroom is an obvious place for them to study. If the student has their own bedroom, advantages include comfort, privacy, and the fact that it's always available.

Disadvantages include the fact that it is not ideal to combine working and sleeping spaces, although few people manage to keep them totally separate. Other places in the home that could be good for learning include the living room, kitchen, or dining room. If your child studies in a room with a television, it should be turned off and perhaps unplugged with the remote control put away, out of reach. Work space options outside the home include school libraries, public libraries, cafés, or outdoor spaces such as parks, whenever the weather is nice. If you haven't done so already, have a conversation with your child and see which of these options appeals to them.

Having three to four options for where to study can help keep a student from feeling trapped or burned out. Parents who homeschool may want to check to see whether their children prefer to learn and study in the same space where teaching occurs or in a different space, and then accommodate them accordingly, if possible.

Handout 10.1 asks your child to express some of these preferences about work space, and Handout 10.2 is a checklist that some students may enjoy customizing and using to make sure they're all set up and ready to go before each round of Focused Study Sessions.

Minds Are Invisible but Brains Are Physical

Since the brain is a part of the body, we need to get enough sleep, good nutrition, and movement in order for our brains to work the very best that they can. One section of Handout 10.1 explores your child's preferences in each of these areas.

Nutrition

Nutrition is a vast subject area that I encourage you to discuss with your child's doctor or a qualified nutritionist. Although it is beyond the scope of this book, I decided to offer some professionally vetted or suggested ideas and resources because nutrition is one of those factors that can make or break a student's learning efforts. Not every student, of course. Future doctors and lawyers have been known to survive for years on ramen noodles. But some students' brains are particularly sensitive to nutrition, and all of them could benefit from optimal nutrition.

The top three things to keep an eye on are iron deficiency, protein intake, and steady blood sugar levels. Low iron means the body has less energy to execute all of its functions, including cognitive processing. If you suspect your child is experiencing brain fog or a lack of energy—even a subtle one—consider having your pediatrician check for anemia, an issue that particularly affects girls. Our brain cells use microscopic messengers to talk to each other, and those messengers are made out of protein. Making sure your child gets enough protein will help their brain cells maintain excellent communication during classes and exams. As for blood sugar levels, the importance of keeping them steady is reflected in our everyday language—"sugar high," "sugar crash," etc. Making sure your child gets enough protein, good fats, and complex carbohydrates will help keep their blood sugar steady so that they can maintain a good energy level throughout the day instead of experiencing mood swings or crashes in focus and concentration. With steady blood sugar levels, they'll be able to crush their eighth period test as easily as their third period one.

For more information about this all-important topic, two books with both nutritional information and recipes are listed in the Recommended Resources.

Movement

In addition to nutrition, movement is crucial for our brain health. Although popular entertainment culture pits dense jocks against weakling geniuses, scientific evidence supports the claim that physical fitness promotes all kinds of brain function including planning (also called *executive functioning*), memory, learning, mood, and stress management.[15] It is most important that your child *enjoys* whatever fitness activities they are involved in. Kids who aren't so fond of sports may enjoy walking the dog, exploring nature, going to dance classes, rocking out to their own playlists in their room, or moving while they play dance or sports simulation video games. In addition, stretching, taking short walks, or doing short bursts of more intense physical activity during study breaks can refresh and recharge the mind. This would be a convenient way of integrating movement into the learning process itself. Moreover, there's no rule against standing up or moving around while studying. For example, the teaching strategy is a perfect opportunity for your child to stand up and walk around their invisible classroom of imaginary students, or simply move around while talking to themselves.

Sleep

Sleep is vital. Although we can get away with less of it when we are young, and although some people—like ER doctors or high-level politicians—might consistently get away with having as little as four or five hours a night, most people suffer if they do not get enough rest. Adequate sleep makes every system in our body work better, and that also goes for the sleep-deprived ER doctors and politicians. Good sleep hygiene includes ending screen time an hour before bed and sleeping in a dark, cool room. To achieve complete darkness, try turning off all electronics and consider using a sleep mask. Researchers tell us that the ideal temperature for sleeping is 65°F, but some people prefer it warmer. When it is too warm though, you may not sleep soundly and deeply throughout the night, and the body may not have the best chance to go through its healing and memory storage processes. You can find out more about the magic of sleep in Matthew Walker's *Why We Sleep*, listed in the Recommended Resources (page 189).

Handout Roundup for Chapter 10

Setting Up: Time Management, Workspace, and Brain Health

Information about the handout roundups can be found in chapter 8 (page 101).

- Handout 10.1: Study Preferences

    — This worksheet investigates your child's preferences about where and how they like to study, how they want to keep themselves distraction-free, and how they'd like to keep their brains ready and raring to go.

— I recommend reading the first section aloud and then giving your child five to ten minutes to quietly fill out the worksheet. Then discuss their answers, and share information from the chapter to help them with any questions that may have stumped them, especially in the sleep section.

— Keep this worksheet for reference, knowing that their preferences may change at any time.

— Schedule a time to follow up with their plans to eliminate distractions on their device(s).

— This worksheet should take 10 to 15 minutes.

- Handout 10.2: Study Session Checklist

  — This handout is a customizable checklist that some students may find helpful to use before their Focused Study Sessions.

  — Give this handout to your child *only* if you think it will be helpful to them and not a tool of procrastination.

- Handout 10.3: Rocks in a Bucket

  — Give your child this handout after doing the exercise described in the chapter (page 126) with them.

  — Ask your child to explain each of the images on the handout to you as they relate to time management. They should emphasize the importance of scheduling high-priority things first, and also being able to find small pockets of time to do small bits of work.

  — If you feel comfortable, share a couple of your own time-management struggles.

  — It should take about 5 to 10 minutes, depending on how much discussion it prompts.

- Handout 10.4: Filling Out Your Term Calendar

  — This handout explains how to fill out a Term Calendar using class syllabi.

  — Have your child read this handout, preferably aloud. If you can extend the session, go ahead and sit with your child while they fill in this calendar using their syllabi. If you cannot extend the session, and you think your child needs the accountability, go ahead and schedule another time to sit with them while they fill it in.

  — This handout should take 5 minutes or less to discuss. Filling out the calendar will take 15 to 25 minutes.

- Handout 10.5: Filling Out Your Weekly Calendar

  — This handout explains how to fill out a Weekly Calendar.

  — Have your child read this handout, preferably aloud. If you can extend the session, go ahead and sit with your child while they fill in this calendar. If you cannot extend the session, and you think your child needs the accountability, go ahead and sit with them at a later time while they fill it in.

  — If it's appropriate, make an agreement with your child to sit and fill in your calendars together at a designated time each week.

  — Make sure your child understands how important it is to start homework as soon as it is assigned.

  — This handout should take 5 minutes or less to discuss. Filling out the calendar will take 5 to 15 minutes, depending on the week in question.

- Handout 10.6: App Detox

  — This worksheet lays out a step-by-step procedure for weaning off time-sucking apps.

  — If your child is currently struggling with too much screen time, gently read through the worksheet with them, and make an agreement about when the detox will begin.

  — It should take 5 to 10 minutes to fill out steps 1 and 2 of this worksheet.

- Handout 10.7: Quiz: Saying No, Setting Boundaries, and Protecting Your Time

  — This is a worksheet modeled on a fun magazine quiz. Each multiple-choice question has three answers. Choice "a" always represents someone who says yes too easily; choice "b" represents someone who has good boundaries; and choice "c" represents someone who is overprotective of their time.

  — Whenever you give this worksheet to your child, have a lively discussion with them about it. Explore the nuances of how they feel about different options. They will probably come up with some great insights.

  — I know that it's easy to see that "b" is the "right" choice for each question. The point is not so much to get accurate answers from your child but to show them several different possible ways of protecting their time while having a social life.

  — This worksheet should take 5 to 15 minutes, depending on how much discussion it prompts.

Chapter 10 Handout Breakdown

For chapter 10, all of the handouts are only available online, but they don't contain any information you need to understand this chapter. Whenever you're ready, the handouts will be waiting for you on the website.

NAME	TITLE
Handout 10.1	Study Preferences Worksheet
Handout 10.2	Study Session Checklist
Handout 10.3	Rocks in a Bucket
Handout 10.4	Filling Out Your Term Calendar
Handout 10.5	Filling Out Your Weekly Calendar
Handout 10.6	App Detox Worksheet
Handout 10.7	Quiz: Saying No, Setting Boundaries, and Protecting Your Time

Action Roundup for Students

I've called this chapter an "action roundup" because it consists entirely of handouts, and most of them focus on practical action rather than ideas. The handouts also combine and integrate ideas from multiple chapters. There are roughly three categories of resources:

1. Ones that help students prepare for the school year or term

2. Ones that help students track their progress throughout the year or term

3. Ones that students can grab whenever they need a lifeline

Handout Roundup for Chapter 11

Action Roundup for Students

Information about the handout roundups can be found in chapter 8 (page 101).

I. PREPARING FOR THE YEAR OR TERM

- Handout 11.1: What Gets You Fired Up Deep Down Inside?

  — I just told you how practical and action-oriented this chapter is, and the first worksheet you read about has the words "deep down inside" in the title? What gives? You may remember that the first question that determines a person's motivation is, "Do I find this goal important?" So it is actually very practical to tie schoolwork as closely as possible to your child's values, goals, and dreams. To account for the fact that different activities motivate different types of students, Handout 11.1 is divided into three parts. In Part I, your child chooses an unlimited number of values and professional goals from provided lists, and then they write down some dreams and aspirations they may have. Part II is an optional exercise where they use their imagination to envision a future for themselves. In Part III, they have the opportunity to create a vision board (or journal or short film, etc.)

concretely depicting the life they want to create for themselves. It's fine to stick to Part I to begin with. The other parts will be there if you want to do them later.

— How long this worksheet takes depends on many factors. Here are my best estimates. Part I: 5–10 minutes; Part II: 10–15 minutes; Part III: 20–30+ minutes

- Handout 11.2: Mapping Out Your Year

  — This worksheet asks students to list the main learning strategies and tools they want to use for most or all of their classes during the year. Suggestions are given. Then it asks them to tie each of their classes to one of their values or goals in a large table. The table also has space for them to list, for each class, (a) which Bloom's level of learning they believe they will need to reach, (b) any extra strategies and tools they will need for the class, and (c) people they can go to for help.

  — This worksheet should take 5 minutes or less to introduce and about 15 to 20 minutes to fill out.

- Handout 11.3: Getting the Most Out of a Syllabus

  — This worksheet guides your child through a four-step process of learning everything they can from a syllabus. Step 1 is to list any questions that they have about the class. Example questions are suggested. Step 2 is to find the answers to their questions on the syllabus and write them down. Space is provided on the handout. Step 3 is to ask you about any of the questions they're having trouble answering. Step 4 is to ask their teacher any remaining questions they may have. Tips for meeting with the teacher are given.

  — To introduce this worksheet, have your child read it aloud.

  — It should take 5 minutes or less to introduce. When your child uses it to explore a syllabus, it should take about 10 to 15 minutes for the first syllabus, and then 5 to 10 minutes for every syllabus after the first.

- Handout 11.4: Procrastination Busters

  — This handout lists seven strategies for breaking through procrastination. I could have put it with the third group of "emergency rescue" resources, but if your child really struggles with procrastination, it will be useful to give them some strategies to prepare for the year.

  — I recommend having your child read it aloud and discussing any strategy they have questions about.

  — Be aware that two of the strategies—breaking things down into smaller steps and using countdowns—might backfire for some students. If they somehow end up with 20 sub-steps or discover that they have 20 paragraphs left to read, they might respond to that by getting overwhelmed and giving up immediately instead of thinking, "OK, this is eventually going to end." You have to judge how you think your child will respond and skip one or both of these strategies if they aren't a good fit.

— This handout should take 5 to 10 minutes to read through and discuss.

II. TRACKING PROGRESS DURING THE YEAR OR TERM

- Handout 11.5: Exam Wrappers

  — This worksheet asks your child to reflect on how they prepared for a recently returned test. They are asked to explore in detail what worked, what didn't work, and how they will prepare even better for the next test. They should use it with every test that is returned to them.

  — The worksheet refers to the Test Preparation Guide, which is Appendix A (page 153) of this book.

  — It also refers to Handout 9.5, A Process for Dealing with Negative Feedback or Failure, which is only appropriate to use with this Exam Wrappers worksheet if your child was devastated by their performance on the test.

  — If your child has one or more classes where the teacher never returns tests, tell them to request a meeting with the teacher to go over the test. Details about this recommendation appear in Appendix A. After the meeting, your child should have enough information to use this worksheet.

  — This worksheet should take 5 minutes or less to introduce. It should take 10 to 30 minutes to use with a returned exam.

- Handout 11.6: Learning Strategies Inventory

  — This handout is a great way to quickly make clear to a student that their grade is connected to *what they are doing* to prepare for a class. It asks students to answer a series of questions about their studying and learning activities for a class, and then it predicts their grade in the class. It was designed for college students, so a lot of high schoolers may be able to do less than the handout says is necessary and still get great grades. However, the handout does prepare students to know what will be required of them in college, and it also very handily makes the point that a student's *behavior* is the primary determiner of their grades.

  — Because this handout was designed for college students, use it only if you think it's a good fit for your child.

  — It takes less than 5 minutes to complete for each class.

- Handout 11.7: Strategies and Tools Tracker

  — This worksheet is a progress tracking table that asks your child to rate, on a scale of 1 to 5, how various tools and strategies are working in different classes. Updating this worksheet every month should give your child a good idea of what's working for them and what could be working better.

  — It should take less than 5 minutes to introduce and 10 to 25 minutes to use every month as a progress tracker.

III. LOOKING FOR A LIFELINE DURING THE YEAR OR TERM

- Handout 11.8: When Overwhelm Strikes

  — In this book, I have given you a super-sized arsenal of strategies and tools because I want to help as many different kinds of students as possible. But I recognize that having too many options can sometimes feel more paralyzing than having none at all! I designed this handout so that your child has a clear directive at any time: *Use note-taking and the teaching strategy to do a 30-minute Focused Study Session.* The handout does give them the freedom to choose a different strategy or tool if they want to.

  Of course, you can also be the human version of this handout and ask your child at any time:

    "What strategy do you want to use right now?"

    "What tool do you want to use?"

    "How long is your Focused Study Session going to be?"

  Then send them to their study area with an encouraging "Woo-hoo!" or a fist pump. Or bump. Or whatever your child finds motivating.

  — This handout should take 1–2 minutes to introduce during a session, and it should take under a minute to use as a lifeline. In other words, it should take under a minute to go through steps 1 and 2 and then sit down for the Focused Study Session.

- Handout 11.9: Quick Reference List of All Learning Support Tools

  — This resource is simply a list of useful reference materials, such as Handout 4.5: Bloom's Levels of Learning and Handout 5.3: Study Cycle with Focused Study Sessions.

  — Use this handout to print a collection of materials your child can keep in a booklet or folder to remind them what you covered during your sessions.

  — There are two lists on the handout: *essential* and *recommended*. Work with your child to decide what should actually go in their booklet or folder.

— It should take less than 5 minutes to introduce this handout and then another 5 to 10 minutes, at some point during or after the session, to print or gather the materials.

You're Almost at the Finish Line

In the next and final chapter, I'll give you a detailed road map for how to deliver the Core Content to your child. Give yourself a round of applause. You've reached the home stretch.

Chapter 11 Handout Breakdown

The table in this breakdown shows chapter 11 handouts, which can all be found online at www.studyandlearn.guide.

NAME	TITLE
Handout 11.1	Worksheet—What Gets You Fired Up Deep Down Inside?
Handout 11.2	Mapping Out Your Year
Handout 11.3	Getting the Most Out of a Syllabus
Handout 11.4	Procrastination Busters
Handout 11.5	Exam Wrappers
Handout 11.6	Learning Strategies Inventory
Handout 11.7	Strategies and Tools Tracker
Handout 11.8	When Overwhelm Strikes
Handout 11.9	Quick Reference List of All Learning Support Resources

CHAPTER 12

Action Roundup for Parents

A Framework for Delivering These Strategies and Ideas to Your Child

In this chapter, I will show you how to lead your child through the material you've just learned in this book.

In the following sections we'll talk about:

1. What content to present to your child

2. A process for presenting the content that works for your family's schedule

3. What to do if your child is struggling *right now*

4. What to do if your child is resistant to the idea of using simple strategies

What Content Should I Share with My Child?

There is a core selection of material in this book that I consider to be essential, and I refer to it as the *Core Content*. To give you a feel for what the Core Content contains, it's useful to recall that the book is roughly split into two parts: Chapters 3–6 cover the nuts and bolts of thinking, learning, and studying, while Chapters 7–10 cover mindset, emotions, and time management—all of the stuff *surrounding* the learning process that can make or break it. You can think of the content in the second half of the book as a key that unlocks the effectiveness of the content in the first part.

PART 1:

Thinking, Learning, & Studying
Chapters 3–6

PART 2:

Mindset, Motivation, & Planning
Chapters 7–10

The Core Content contains *all* of the Part 1 material plus the Part 2 material that, in my experience, makes the most difference for students. So I strongly recommend that you present the Core Content to your child in full.

The material that is not in the Core Content is referred to as *Additional Content*, and all of it comes from Part 2 of the book. The next two sections list exactly the resources that each "bucket" of content contains. Please keep in mind that for your particular child, something in the Additional Content might be crucial, for example the App Detox or Procrastination Busters handouts. To sum up, I recommend delivering all of the Core Content to your child and whatever Additional Content you think suits their needs or could be a game changer for them.

Core Content

The following table is organized by chapter and lists everything you need to present the Core Content to your child. The scripts, script summaries, handout roundups, and answer keys are in this book, and the table shows exactly where you can find them. All of the handouts are on the website. Estimated time frames for how long each chapter will take you to move through are also given with each chapter heading in the table. I think it will be convenient for most parents to deliver two to four chapters of material in one sitting. We'll get into scheduling in more detail shortly.

The following table is reproduced in Handout 12.1, available on the website, for your convenience.

CORE CONTENT (with book page references as well as time frame suggestions per chapter)

RESOURCE	LOCATION	TITLE
Chapter 3: *10–20 mins*		**Metacognition**
Ch 3 Script	pp. 25–28	—
Ch 3 Script Summary	29	—
Handout 3.1	web	Who is Dr. McGuire and Why Should I Care About What She Says?
Handout 3.2	web	What is Metacognition and How Can It Help Me?
Handout 3.3	web	Count the Vowels
Handout 3.4	web	Metacognition Worksheet
Answer Key 3.4A	31–33	Answer Key for Metacognition Worksheet
Chapter 4: *15–20 mins*		**Bloom's Levels Of Learning**
Ch 4 Script	35–38	—
Ch 4 Script Summary	39	—
Handout 4.1	web	Answering Reflection Questions
Handout 4.2	web	Other Students' Answers to Reflection Question #1
Handout 4.3	web	Other Students' Answers to Reflection Question #3
Handout 4.4	web	Alternative Answers to Reflection Question #3
Handout 4.5	web	Bloom's Levels of Learning
Handout 4.6	web	Bloom's Levels of Learning: Goldilocks Edition
Answer Key 4.6A	43	Answer Key for Bloom's Levels of Learning: Goldilocks Edition
Chapter 5: *5–10 mins*		**The Study Cycle**
Ch 5 Script	46–48	—
Ch 5 Script Summary	49–50	—
Handout 5.1	web	The Study Cycle
Handout 5.2	web	Focused Study Sessions
Handout 5.3	web	The Study Cycle and Focused Study Sessions Combined
Chapter 6: *30–35 mins*		**Ten Learning Strategies**
Ch 6 Script	56–62	—
Ch 6 Script Summary	64–66	—
Handout 6.1	web	Guess the Activity/The Power of Previewing
Handout 6.2	web	Using Your Homework to Test Your Understanding
Handout 6.3	web	Ten Learning Strategies
Handout 6.4	web	Learning Strategies Worksheet
Handout 6.5	web	Quick Reference: List of Study Tools

(continued)

Core Content (continued)

RESOURCE	LOCATION	TITLE
Chapter 7: *20–25 mins*		**Mindset**
Ch 7 Script	72–76	—
Ch 7 Script Summary	77–78	—
Handout 7.1	web	Fixed and Growth Mindsets
Handout 7.2	web	Mindset Worksheet
Answer Key 7.2A	82	Answer Key for Select Questions on Mindset Worksheet
Chapter 8: *25 mins*		**Motivation**
Ch 8 Handout Roundup	102–103	—
Handout 8.2	web	Worksheet about My Interests and Things I Enjoy Doing
Handout 8.3	web	How Do You Prefer to Learn? (Worksheet)
Handout 8.4	web	How to Figure Out What You Are Actually Supposed to Be Doing
Chapter 9: *15–25 mins*		**Dealing With Failure**
Ch 9 Handout Roundup	117–118	—
Handout 9.2	web	Dealing with Setbacks, Mistakes, and Failure
Handout 9.4	web	Mistakes and Failure Worksheet
Answer Key 9.4A	122–123	Answer Key for Mistakes and Failure Worksheet
Chapter 10: *15–30 mins*		**Planning And Time Management**
Ch 10 Handout Roundup	132–133	—
Handout 10.1	web	Study Preferences Worksheet
Handout 10.3	web	Rocks in a Bucket
Handout 10.4	web	Filling Out Your Term Calendar
Handout 10.5	web	Filling Out Your Weekly Calendar
Chapter 11: *15–30 mins*		**Action Roundup For Students**
Ch 11 Handout Roundup	135–139	—
Handout 11.1	web	What Gets You Fired Up Deep Down Inside? PART I ONLY
Handout 11.2	web	Mapping Out Your Year
Handout 11.3	web	Getting the Most Out of a Syllabus
Handout 11.5	web	Exam Wrappers
Handout 11.8	web	When Overwhelm Strikes
Handout 11.9	web	Quick Reference List of All Learning Support Resources
Appendix A	web	Test Preparation Guide

Additional Content

The following table organizes the Additional Content according to chapter and gives an estimated time frame for each handout, as opposed to each chapter. Since you might choose one or more of these handouts to go through with your child as a stand-alone activity, or add them to a Core Content session, the timing per handout is useful for you to know. This table is reproduced in Handout 12.2, available on the website, for your reference.

ADDITIONAL CONTENT (with book page references as well as time frame suggestions per handout)

RESOURCE	LOCATION	TITLE (TIMING)
Chapter 8		**Motivation**
Ch 8 Handout Roundup	pp. 102–103	—
Handout 8.5	web	Self-Talk Journaling Worksheet (5–10 mins)
Handout 8.6	web	Doing What *You* Can and Letting Go of the Rest (10–20 mins)
Chapter 9		**Dealing With Failure**
Ch 9 Handout Roundup	117–118	—
Handout 9.3	web	Stumbling Blocks or Stepping Stones? (5 mins)
Handout 9.5	web	A Process for Dealing with Negative Feedback or Failure (10 mins to introduce)
Handout 9.6	web	Worksheet—Defining Success (5–10 mins)
Chapter 10		**Planning and Time Management**
Ch 10 Handout Roundup	132–133	—
Handout 10.2	web	Study Session Checklist (1–5 mins)
Handout 10.6	web	App Detox Worksheet (5–10 mins to introduce)
Handout 10.7	web	Quiz: Saying No, Setting Boundaries, and Protecting Your Time (5–15 mins)
Chapter 11		**Action Roundup for Students**
Chapter 11 Handout Roundup	135–138	—
Handout 11.1	web	What Gets You Fired Up Deep Down Inside? PARTS II and III (20 mins or more)
Handout 11.4	web	Procrastination Busters (5–10 mins)
Handout 11.6	web	Learning Strategies Inventory (2–5 mins to introduce)
Handout 11.7	web	Strategies and Tools Tracker (2–5 mins to introduce)
Appendix B		
Appendix B	web	Study Tools Guide

When and How Should I Present the Content to My Child?

I hope that looking at the Core Content and Additional Content tables makes it easy to imagine sitting down with your child to go through a few chapters of content at a time. The most important thing, so that the key can turn the lock, is to keep up the momentum so they get the Core Content as a package. Try to deliver it within one to two weeks total, within one week if you can. Keeping up the momentum is also important because the sooner you finish going through the Core Content, the sooner your child is likely to start seeing results. And it's their progress and success that will motivate them to continue using the strategies. Recall the cycle of motivation from chapter 1:

To consider one possible schedule, if you present the materials from chapters 3–5 one day, chapters 6–7 another day, chapters 8–9 a third day, and chapters 10–11 a fourth day, you will have moved through the material at a brisk pace, likely within a week. Or if you happen to have 90 minutes on a Saturday or Sunday morning, you could present all the materials through chapters 3–6, so that you've delivered the learning strategies in chapter 6 by the end of that first sit-down session. Other divisions of the Core Content are certainly appropriate, including going through the materials from one chapter per night if that's what will work best for you and your family. As long as you get to the end of the chapter you're working on by the end of your session, you're good to go.

If you happen to be a homeschooling parent with full control over your lesson plans, you may decide that you want to present all of the material—Core and Additional Content— together right off the bat and do an entire unit on learning.

For parents who like to use planning tools, I've provided Handout 12.3 to help you map out exactly when you will sit down with your child and the chapters you will cover during those sessions. But if that feels burdensome, forget the handout and just do what feels right for you and your family.

Here is a summary of the guiding principles when deciding how to present the content:

- Have a clear overview of the material, best accomplished by reading the entire book and all of the web handouts before working with your child.

- Focus on the Core Content to begin with, plus whatever Additional Content you think could be useful for your child.

- Maintain momentum and try to finish the whole process within a week or two.

- During each session, get to the end of a chapter.

- Remember that whatever you don't cover in depth, including the Additional Content, you can return to that material at a later time.

- If life gets in the way, no worries. Just pick up the process when you can. Better late than never.

- Follow-up is key. After delivering the Core Content, check in with your child briefly but consistently, every couple of weeks, about their use of the learning strategies.

Return to the Resources in This Book as Long as Your Children Are in School

You can use this book like a cookbook, returning to it again and again throughout your child's education for fresh ideas and inspiration, depending on what they have an "appetite" for in a particular moment. For example, every time your child gets an exam back, they can use Handout 11.5: Exam Wrappers. Any time they're struggling with an assignment, they can take a look at Handout 8.4: How to Figure Out What You Are Actually Supposed to Be Doing, or perhaps Handout 11.4: Procrastination Busters, or maybe even Handout 11.8: When Overwhelm Strikes. I hope they will use Handout 11.2: Mapping Out Your Year before every school year.

Appendix D, the Handout Index, lists several common situations students find themselves in and a selection of handouts to address them. You can use it once you've led your child through the Core Content. Appendix E is a complete list of all of the handouts, answer keys, and guides, organized by chapter, for your reference. My sincere wish is that the wide selection of resources in this book will become more and more useful to you over time.

In Case of Emergency Break Glass

If your child is currently in academic crisis and you know that they could benefit from a particular strategy in chapter 6, go ahead and share it with them out of context. Although I don't generally recommend breaking up the complete package of my method, there's no doubt that doing so can work under specific circumstances. The first part of Appendix D is devoted to urgent situations. Start there—or simply with one strategy you've already recognized as potentially transformative for your child—if they have something urgent coming up in a day or two. Once the crisis has passed, then circle back and lead them through all of the Core Content.

The main reason not to give your child handouts out of context *unless* they're facing an emergency is that presenting the Core Content in order gives you the best shot at providing your child what they need to reach their full potential over the long haul.

My Child Resists the Idea that Simple Ideas Can Be Helpful

Sometimes students are convinced that they don't need learning strategies. In fact, this is the reason I commonly recommend that college teachers don't arrange a strategies presentation for their students until after the results of the first exam have been returned and the students have hard evidence that they need to do something different.

Do what you think is best based on your child's personality. If you think they're open to trying something new right now, then go ahead and plan to lead them through the Core Content as soon as possible. If you have a more stubborn or overconfident child, perhaps it's worth letting them flail a little bit before you offer them a lifeline.

You might consider mentioning to your child, "I learned about these really helpful strategies you could use to study smarter, not necessarily harder, and I think you would really like them." If your invitation gets a chilly reception, then maybe wait until your child experiences an academic disappointment to ask them again. Judge the timing according to what you know about your child.

A Brief Word about Branding: Boring Study Skills versus Exciting Learning Strategies

Especially if your child is stubborn or overconfident, you may want to avoid the term *study skills*, which many students think are boring and useless. In my experience, when a confident student hears that you're going to teach them some powerful study skills, they can barely suppress their eyeroll. But if you say you're going to share some *metacognitive learning strategies*, then they perk up and get interested.

Handout Roundup for Chapter 12: Action Roundup for Parents

- Handout 12.1 summarizes the *Core Content* I recommend all parents present to their children, for easy reference.

- Handout 12.2 summarizes the *Additional Content* you may want to share with your child.

- Handout 12.3 is an optional scheduling worksheet you can use to map out specific dates when you will go through specific content with your child. There is no need to use it if you prefer to be spontaneous.

- Handout 12.4 is a tool for setting clear expectations for your child for the term or year. It is included only if you find that it will work for your family. Otherwise, skip it.

Confident, Independent Learning for a Lifetime

Thank you for coming on this journey of learning and discovery with me. Hats off to you for investing your time and energy to give your child something that no one can take away from them—foundational skills they will use for their entire lives. When students are empowered to independently resolve learning challenges, it can open up new horizons for them, far beyond their schoolwork.

I wish you the best in your journey toward turning your child into an expert learner. In the meantime, I'll be waving my pompoms.

Chapter 12 Handout Breakdown

All handouts except the answer keys are available on the website. The table in this breakdown shows all chapter 12 handouts. **The handouts also reproduced in the book are shown in bold.**

NAME	TITLE
Handout 12.1	Core Content
Handout 12.2	Additional Content
Handout 12.3	**Scheduling Your Sessions with Your Child and Other Check-Ins**
Handout 12.4	**Setting Clear Expectations for the Year**

Handouts 12.1–12.2 are available on the website.

They are not crucial for understanding the book's content as you read it, but you will use them during your sessions with your child and may want to know what they contain. If so, go to www.studyandlearn.guide.

HANDOUT 12.3   Scheduling Your Sessions with Your Child and Other Check-Ins

	DATE	CHAPTERS
Session 1:		
Session 2:		
Session 3:		
Session 4:		
Session 5:		

Dates for beginning digital detox or a session for disabling all notifications: _____

Have we ordered a stand-alone timer? _____

Dates for Progress Check-Ins throughout the year (there are nine slots for nine months):

_____   _____   _____

_____   _____   _____

_____   _____   _____

HANDOUT 12.4 Setting Clear Expectations for the Year

In Chapter 8, we learned about the importance of setting clear expectations. Here's a tool for you to work through your own expectations before presenting them to your child, perhaps just before the beginning of the school year. When you present them, make sure your child knows it's because you love them and want the best for them. If it's appropriate, give them some room to negotiate. You can use this tool at the start of every school year or term.

School Year or Term: _____

After thinking carefully about my child's load of classes, extracurricular activities, and family obligations, I expect them to maintain at least this minimum average: _____.

Feel free to express the average as a letter grade (with or without plus or minus), a number out of 100, or a number out of 4.0.

I expect my child to spend approximately _____ hours a week with their schoolwork.

The consequences for not maintaining the minimum average will be: _____

_____

_____

_____

The rewards for exceeding _____ average will be: _____

_____

_____

_____

What does my child complain most about regarding their family and household obligations? Is there a way for me to use cutting them some slack in that area as a reward for something else? _____

_____

_____

Test Preparation Guide

Testing Tips

Before the test

1. Use the learning strategies in Chapter 6 and do homework as soon as it is assigned.

2. Find out what types of questions will be on the test and practice those types of questions. If you know you might have to write an essay about the events that started World War I, practice writing that essay. If you know you could be asked to solve four different types of trigonometry proofs, spend time mastering each type.

3. Prepare a study guide by organizing the information you need to master into charts, tables, outlines, timelines, or mind maps. If you want more information, see #5 of Appendix B: Study Tools Guide.

4. Set aside time slots to prepare for your test. Practice doing the questions or problems as quickly as you will be expected to do them during the test. If you typically run out of time on tests, figure out about how much time you will have for the different kinds of questions or problems. If you have trouble, talk to your teacher. Then use a timer, and practice doing the questions in the time that you will be given. See Handout 11.4: Procrastination Busters for more information about timers and how they can help you study.

5. Add to this list other suggestions from teachers, friends, and other sources.

On test day

1. Quickly write down any formulas, dates, or other memorized information you may need before you begin. (Only do this if you are 100 percent certain that this strategy will not be judged as cheating. I have heard stories of students who are not allowed to write anything but answers on their test papers.)

2. *Carefully* read directions, pay attention to any extra instructions from your teacher, and ask questions if you have them.

3. Quickly look over the whole test before you begin so that you can make sure not to spend too much time on any one question.

4. Expect that you will forget some things. Don't sweat it. If it happens, move on to other questions, and be confident that the information will come back to you as you continue working through the test.

5. If you are feeling very anxious, inhale while you slowly count to 4, and exhale while you count to 4. (If you want more ideas about how to regularly practice deep breathing, do an internet search and see which techniques and recommendations work best for you.)

6. Remind yourself that you are prepared, and that you can do this.

7. Add to this list other suggestions from teachers, friends, and other sources.

After the test

1. Congratulate yourself for doing your best and give yourself some kind of reward.

2. Once you get the test back, take a closer look at how you did and what you can do better next time, using Handout 11.5: Exam Wrappers.*

3. If you were really disappointed with how you did on the test and feel scared about looking at it, use Handout 9.5: A Process for Dealing with Negative Feedback or Failure to help yourself ease into it.

4. If your tests are not returned to you, then as soon as possible after you receive your grade, ask your teacher to meet with you. Explain that you would like to see which questions you answered incorrectly so that you can do better on the next test. At the meeting, take detailed notes about the questions you missed. Then do Handout 11.5: Exam Wrappers, using your notes.

* A learning strategist named Marsha Lovett at Carnegie Mellon University created this technique.

Study Tools Guide

Study Tools: What to Do During Focused Study Sessions

This guide is an expanded version of Handout 6.5: Quick Reference List of Study Tools. It lists study activities that you can do during your Focused Study Sessions. I have chosen the ones that are popular with students I know, but please keep in mind that there are other useful study tools that do not appear on this list. If you want some more ideas, talk to your teachers. Your friends might have additional ideas.

Please be aware that there are ideas and examples here for a wide range of levels, from freshmen all the way to seniors, in order to make it useful for the most students. If you are just starting high school, don't worry if some of the examples seem difficult. Just focus on using the learning strategies, and in a few years, you'll understand everything in this packet.

1. Making Flashcards

Flashcards are perfect for memorizing information like vocabulary words, names, dates, geographical facts, and formulas. Making flashcards by hand with index cards can be fun, but you can also use flashcard-making software that you can find online.

2. Taking Notes While You Read

There are many different ways to take notes, so if you don't already have a system that works, you may have to try out several different ways in order to find out what works best for you.

Note-taking Method #1: Taking Notes While You Paraphrase

The first note-taking method I'll suggest is based on the reading strategy you've already learned: Put What You Are Reading into Your Own Words. I'll briefly remind you how it works. Let's say you are reading a section of a textbook. Using this method, you start at the beginning and read the first paragraph. Then you summarize what you've just read in your own words, either out loud or in your head. Next you read the second paragraph and put it into your own words *as you also fold in information from paragraph 1*, again, either out loud or in your head. Next you read the third paragraph and put it into your own words, *as you also fold in information from paragraphs 1 and 2*. You continue in this way until the end of the section, and when the next section begins, you start fresh with only the first paragraph of that section. The point of this method is to make sure you understand each section *as a whole* and are able to see the big picture and access deeper insights whenever you read. It's a way of getting you to higher levels of learning (see Handout 4.5).

But how does this method work with note-taking? As you put what you are reading into your own words, write some or all of it down. You will be adding new *information* and new *insights* into your written notes as you progress through the material, even though you will be paraphrasing from the beginning of the section. That's it.

Note-taking Method #2: Outlining

Another, slightly more advanced option is to take notes by outlining. With this method, you use traditional Roman numerals (I, II, III) to represent the broadest organizational level of information, capital letters (A, B, C) to represent the next level, and numbers (1, 2, 3) for the next level.

Has an English teacher ever asked you to outline a big writing project in this way? This is like doing that, but backwards. It's like playing detective to imagine what outline the textbook writer was using when they wrote the book. Making an outline can give you deep insight into how the information you are trying to learn is structured and organized. Outlining can get even more detailed, so if this technique appeals to you, go ahead and do an internet search to learn more about it.

Note-taking Method #3: Cornell Notes

If you want to take note-taking one step further, you can do an internet search on the Cornell note-taking system. It's a system developed by learning specialist named Walter Pauk. Two helpful videos appear on website of Cornell University's Learning Strategies Center, and I recommend you start with them.

If You Don't Know Which Method to Try, Keep It Simple

Remember you can always start with method #1 and jot things down as you paraphrase. Or just take free-form notes.

You Can Doodle or Sketch as You Take Notes

Whichever way you decide to do take notes, don't forget about the value of making little drawings while you take notes, especially if you like to doodle. If there are ideas or information that are easier to represent with a picture or a little graph, just go ahead and draw it. For example, if you're studying the French Revolution, "Maximilien Robespierre masterminded the Reign of Terror from 1792-1794 before being executed at the guillotine in 1794" is just as clearly expressed by "M. Robespierre ➔ Reign of Terror 1792-1794. MR 🪦 💀 in 1794." Doodles and drawings can also be useful in math and science classes when you have to draw models, graphs, or molecular structure. Of course, writing more fleshed-out notes can help you practice important skills if your tests involve short-answer or essay questions.

Pen & Paper or Keyboard?

Finally, there's the question of whether to take notes by hand or use a keyboard or other digital device. There are good arguments for both, so experiment and see what seems to work best for you. Taking notes by hand may be better for learning because it forces you to put things into your own words. But typed notes may be easier to review later. Of course, it matters if *you* have a big preference for one over the other because if you really dislike taking notes in a particular way, you'll be less likely to do it, no matter how good it might be for learning. You should feel free to use the method you prefer.

The bottom line is: always do what you think will work best for you, and stay open to trying other options if you find your first choice isn't working the way you want it to.

3. Highlighting

If your reading assignments are online or digital, it is often possible to highlight the text in different colors. If you are reading books or handouts, and you know you definitely have permission to mark them up, then you can use highlighter pens of different colors. For example, if you are learning about the Civil War in U.S. History, you might highlight the names of all Union politicians and military officials in blue and use a different color for those in the Confederacy. Color coding can be an efficient way to remind yourself how information is organized into different categories. One note of caution: don't use highlighting as a way of passively marking information "to learn later on." Instead, use it to actively support your use of the reading strategies.

4. Using Visuals: Mind Maps, Charts, Tables, and Timelines

Mind Maps

Mind mapping, or concept mapping, is a popular way of organizing information that may be harder to represent by writing lines of words. Mind mapping allows you to represent information, ideas, or events visually, and even in pictures. A mind map is created by putting the main concept or topic in the center of your map and then drawing branches from the central topic to several main ideas about the topic. You can continue drawing branches from each of the main ideas, and you can even represent connections between ideas with additional arrows.

Diagram B.1 shows a map of the Civil Rights Movement that a junior or senior might make while studying for an American history class. The main ideas branching off from the central idea are (1) the circumstances and conditions that led to the movement, (2) major activist events, (3) important court cases, (4) federal legislation that resulted, and (5) a selection of important organizations and figures. The student who created this map had to reach level 4 of Bloom's pyramid, *Analyzing*, in order to organize events from different time periods into overarching categories. *Having* the map is useful for review, but *creating* the map is what allows this student to enjoy the deep, secure learning that will enable them to excel on a test.

What if a student is taking an advanced class like AP U.S. History and needs to include much more detail in their study materials? In that case, online or digital maps are a good choice because they hold unlimited information. Use them for more advanced classes.

Diagram B.1 doesn't contain any images within the map, but mind maps can be particularly great for more visual subjects like geography, biology, or chemistry, where you need to draw lots of molecules, cell components, organs, or other anatomical features.

Charts and Graphs

Ways of visualizing information other than mind maps include flowcharts, bar charts, pie charts, and graphs. Flowcharts are helpful when you want to lay out a process, or something that happens in sequence. They can be useful in science and history classes, and you can also use them for laying out the plots of novels or other kinds of stories. Diagram B.2 shows a flowchart for the process of meiosis, which every high school biology student will need to master at some point. Diagram B.3 shows a bar chart of the gases in Earth's atmosphere, which all earth science students will eventually be tested on. Making charts is a powerful way of helping you learn the information deeply so that it will be there whenever you're asked about it on a test.

Graphs are also great for deep learning. An algebra student might find it very helpful to make a review sheet comparing the graphs for a line ($y = x$), a parabola ($y = x2$), a cubic ($y = x3$), and even higher powers of x. Then they could add some examples of translations ($y = x2 + b$) and dilations ($y = ax3$) and be able to see what the patterns are and how they work.

Tables

Tables are a very popular choice for organizing information. Diagram B.4 shows one for an upper-level English class and Diagram B.5 shows one for an algebra II or pre-calculus class.

Studying a novel is a great opportunity to use a table, as demonstrated by Diagram B.4. The student who created this table had to get to Bloom's level 4, *Analyzing*, in order to create it. Because the student had the goal of creating the table as she read, she took more thoughtful notes and engaged in deeper metacognition. So the table activated her learning in several ways. Having Diagram B.4 as a review tool before a test is just icing on the cake for this student.

Diagram B.5 shows how a table can be used to map out different approaches to solving trigonometric identities. A student using the homework strategy (Handout 6.2) could create this study tool over the course of two or three weeks, as they move through the unit, do more and more of these kinds of problems, and have more *aha* moments. Even after creating the table in its current form, the student can continue filling it in and refining it. But be aware that there are lots of different ways to organize the information in Diagram B.5. The diagram only shows one way. You should always do what feels right for you and the way your brain works!

In short, making tables is as useful as making maps, charts, or graphs when it comes to climbing Bloom's pyramid to higher levels of learning. The act of organizing the information is a powerful metacognitive process that will help your brain remember what it needs when you're taking tests.

Timelines

Finally, timelines are great for learning history, whether it's for an actual history class, for a historical novel in English class, or a sequence of events like the development of atomic models. You can find examples of a timeline in any history textbook or by doing an internet search for timelines.

With all of these visual tools, you have the choice between making your images by hand on paper or going digital and using software and apps. Whatever floats your boat. Ask your friends and teacher for recommendations, experiment, and stay open to your instincts and creativity.

Mapping the Civil Rights Movement

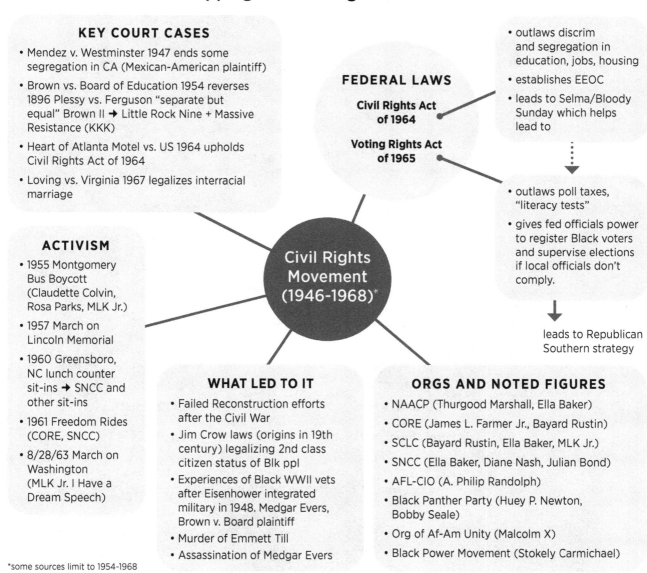

KEY COURT CASES

- Mendez v. Westminster 1947 ends some segregation in CA (Mexican-American plaintiff)
- Brown vs. Board of Education 1954 reverses 1896 Plessy vs. Ferguson "separate but equal" Brown II → Little Rock Nine + Massive Resistance (KKK)
- Heart of Atlanta Motel vs. US 1964 upholds Civil Rights Act of 1964
- Loving vs. Virginia 1967 legalizes interracial marriage

FEDERAL LAWS

Civil Rights Act of 1964

Voting Rights Act of 1965

- outlaws discrim and segregation in education, jobs, housing
- establishes EEOC
- leads to Selma/Bloody Sunday which helps lead to
- outlaws poll taxes, "literacy tests"
- gives fed officials power to register Black voters and supervise elections if local officials don't comply.

leads to Republican Southern strategy

ACTIVISM

- 1955 Montgomery Bus Boycott (Claudette Colvin, Rosa Parks, MLK Jr.)
- 1957 March on Lincoln Memorial
- 1960 Greensboro, NC lunch counter sit-ins → SNCC and other sit-ins
- 1961 Freedom Rides (CORE, SNCC)
- 8/28/63 March on Washington (MLK Jr. I Have a Dream Speech)

Civil Rights Movement (1946-1968)*

WHAT LED TO IT

- Failed Reconstruction efforts after the Civil War
- Jim Crow laws (origins in 19th century) legalizing 2nd class citizen status of Blk ppl
- Experiences of Black WWII vets after Eisenhower integrated military in 1948. Medgar Evers, Brown v. Board plaintiff
- Murder of Emmett Till
- Assassination of Medgar Evers

ORGS AND NOTED FIGURES

- NAACP (Thurgood Marshall, Ella Baker)
- CORE (James L. Farmer Jr., Bayard Rustin)
- SCLC (Bayard Rustin, Ella Baker, MLK Jr.)
- SNCC (Ella Baker, Diane Nash, Julian Bond)
- AFL-CIO (A. Philip Randolph)
- Black Panther Party (Huey P. Newton, Bobby Seale)
- Org of Af-Am Unity (Malcolm X)
- Black Power Movement (Stokely Carmichael)

*some sources limit to 1954-1968

Diagram B.1. An example of a mind map for a junior- or senior-level history class. In order to make this map, this student must create an overview of the Civil Rights Movement, sorting events from various time periods into different categories like "Federal Laws" or "Key Court Cases." This mind map on 8.5 x 11-inch paper is limited in how much detail it shows, but online or digital maps can hold unlimited information and are useful for more advanced classes. A timeline would be another great tool for learning this material.

Meiosis Flowchart

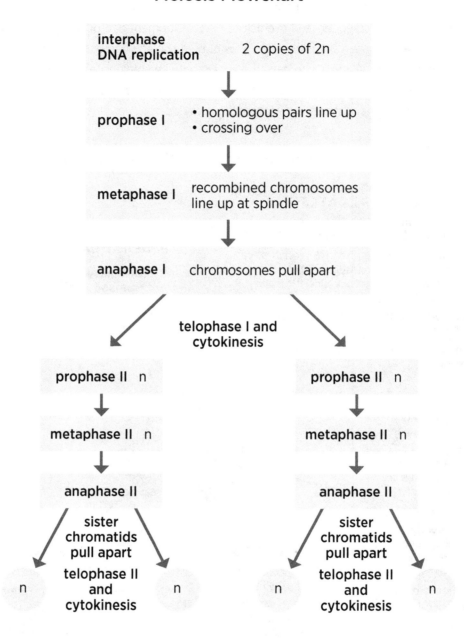

Diagram B.2. An example of a flowchart for a freshman- or sophomore-level biology class. Making this chart without referring to notes helps this student securely learn the process of meiosis.

Bar Chart of Earth's Atmospheric Composition

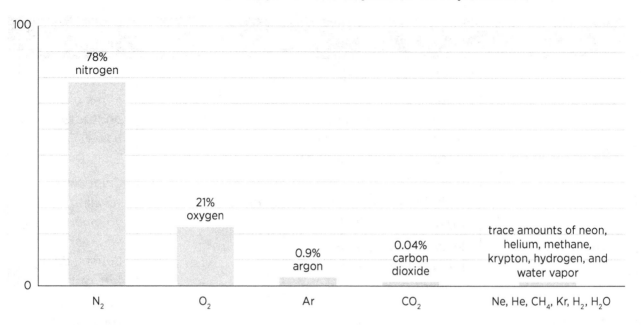

Diagram B.3. An example of a bar chart for a freshman- or sophomore-level earth science class. Making the chart helps the student learn the information securely, and they also have it as a review sheet.

PARTIAL BREAKDOWN OF *PLAGUE OF DOVES* BY LOUISE ERDRICH, SET IN THE FICTIONAL TOWN OF PLUTO, NORTH DAKOTA

NARRATORS & PERSPECTIVES	SYMBOLS & THEMES	LITERARY & HISTORICAL REFS	BACKGROUNDS & LANGUAGES
Generation born ~1950 • Evelina Harp Generation born ~1915 • Judge Antone Coutts • Marn Wolde Generation born ~1890 • Cordelia Lochren Generation born ~1870 • Joseph Coutts • Shamengwa • Mooshum/Seraph Milk (narrates through others' accounts of his storytelling) 3rd person omniscient • Warren Wolde, Billy Peace • John Wildstrand (through Antone Coutts) Others?	Reptiles/Amphibians • salamanders (bred by Harps in backyard pond, almost-killer of Father Cassidy, Evelina's college hallucinations) • Sister Mary Anita called Godzilla by students • Marn Wolde's snake handling symbols of both damnation and salvation Music/Violin • witness to 1888 murders • bond between Henri and Lafayette and their downfall • savior of Joseph Coutts during prospecting winter • savior of Shamengwa and then Corwin Peace • killer of Warren Wolde Religion/Spirituality • Roman Catholicism • Indigenous spiritual traditions • born-again Christianity • new age spirituality • Mormonism • agnostic (Sister Mary Anita)	Greeks & Romans Marcus Aurelius (read by Joseph Coutts, then Antone Coutts, then Evelina) Lucretius Epicetus Plotinus Modern writers (all Evelina) • Anaïs Nin • Albert Camus • Arthur Rimbaud • Sylvia Plath Historical References • Louis Riel (as Michif visionary hero, or as misguided, or as a source of Milk family's and Lafayette's credibility/respect many others. ask for help with this in class.	Backgrounds • Métis (many characters, see below) • French/ Chippewa (Evelina, younger Harps, younger Coutts, Henri, Lafayette) • Chippewa (Milk family) • Cree • Dakota • German • Norwegian Languages • English • Ojibwe • Michif • French Michif - different? • French • German

Diagram B.4. An example of a table for junior- or senior-level English class analyzing the novel *The Plague of Doves* by Louise Erdrich. The student uses the table to organize the different narrators and themes of the book, operating at level 4 of Bloom's pyramid of learning.

Solving Trig Identities

Formulas for Solving Identities (memorize all formulas with flashcards)

- reciprocal identities   example: $1/\sin\theta = \csc\theta$
- Pythagorean identities   example: $\sin^2\theta + \cos^2\theta = 1$
- complementary identities   example: $\cos(\theta - 90) = \sin\theta$
- sum and difference identities   example: $\sin(A \pm B) = \sin A \cos B \pm \cos A \sin B$
- double and half angle identities   example: $\cos^2 A = \cos^2 A - \sin^2 A$
- law of sines
- law of cosines
- algebraic identities   examples: $(a + b)^2 = a^2 + 2ab + b^2$
                          OR $(a+b)^3 = (a + b)(a^2 - ab + b^2)$

Approaches for Solving Identities

IF	THEN
there are squares, cubes, or other powers	try Pythagorean, double angle, or algebraic identities or the cosine rule, depending on what it most looks like
there are angles angle like 75 or 135 (or any angle that's a sum or difference of the common angles)	try one of the sum and difference identities
the expression is similar to the law of sines or the law of cosines	try whichever law it looks like
the expression is similar to an algebraic identity	try whichever one it looks like
there are square roots	try half-angle identities
you get stuck or don't know what to do	convert everything to sines and cosines
you get stuck or don't know what to do	can you convert to a complementary angle?
(general tip)	pick one side to work with, but be aware you might need to work with the other side too
(general tip)	don't move terms from one side to another

Diagram B. 5. An example of a student combining a list and chart to learn how to solve trig identities in a junior- or senior-level class. The *list* shows all the different kinds of formulas they must memorize, at level 1 of Bloom's. The *chart*, however, is level 3 of Bloom's, *Applying*.

5. Making Study Guides

Study guides are great for reviewing information that you have learned over a period of weeks or months while using the other tools. That makes it ideal for test preparation.

Two popular formats for study guides are (1) outlines and (2) tables (sometimes called charts). With both formats, you organize the information from the entire unit into one outline or table. The task of combining and integrating the information makes you go to higher levels of learning on Bloom's pyramid.

You also have the option to create a study guide simply by combining the outlines, maps, tables, charts, or graphs that you created during the unit or chapter. But you may find that your understanding has grown as the unit progressed, and so you need to revise or add to your earlier materials. That revision is a very valuable part of the learning process.

Many textbooks have *learning objectives* or *learning goals* at the beginning or end of every chapter. They may not be labeled with those terms, but they will be introduced with language like, "By the end of this chapter you should be able to..." You can use them to organize your study guides. Turn the objectives into questions, and make sure you have information in your study guide that addresses all of the questions. For example, if your book says: By the end of this chapter you should be able to:

- Explain the states of matter
- Convert grams to moles
- Describe different types of bonding

then your questions would look like this:

- What are the states of matter?
- What is the procedure for converting grams to moles?
- What are all the different types of bonds?

and the section of your study guide for just the *first* question would look like this:

I.   Chapter 1: Matter, Interactions, and Reactions

   A.   Three States of Matter

      1.   Gases: atoms or molecules are far apart, interactions are weak. Gases fill their containers. Examples are water vapor- $H_2O(g)$, methane- $CH_4(g)$, and nitrogen- $N_2(g)$.

      2.   Liquids: atoms or molecules are closer together, interactions are stronger than in gases, weaker than in solids. Liquids take the shape of their containers. Examples are water- $H_2O(l)$, octane- $C_8H_{18}(l)$, and mercury Hg(l).

      3.   Solids: atoms or molecules are very close together, interactions are stronger than in liquids. Solids maintain their shape. Examples are table salt- $NaCl(s)$, calcium carbonate- $CaCO_3(s)$, and diamond- C(s).

Here is an example of a study guide that isn't as helpful:

I. Chapter 1: Matter, Interactions, and Reactions

    A. Know the states of matter

    B. Know how to convert grams to moles

    C. Know the different types of bonding

Although this attempt at a study guide is better than doing nothing, and it makes the student who created it *feel* like they're studying, they're not really engaging deeply with the information so that they can really *learn* it. To get the most out of making study guides, fill them with useful information, and then make sure you can teach that information.

6. Using Mnemonic Devices

Mnemonic device is just a fancy term for a trick that helps you remember something. The name Roy G. Biv is one example. It represents the colors of the rainbow: Red, Orange, Yellow, Green, Blue, Indigo, and Violet. The first letter of each of the colors spells Roy G. Biv. A second example: Dear King Philip Came Over for Great Spaghetti. The first letter of each word in the sentence matches the first letter of each of the taxonomic levels that biology students have to learn: domain, kingdom, phylum, class, order, family, genus, species. The nonsense word IPMAT could help you remember the phases of mitosis: interphase, prophase, metaphase, anaphase, and telophase. Whenever you have to memorize a list of some kind, see if you can come up with a mnemonic device to help you.

7. Creating Practice Quizzes and Tests, with or without Apps

You can use past homework assignments, quizzes, and extra textbook questions to try to create your own practice test. This is an advanced study strategy, but it can work really well. A slightly easier option is to use an app to quiz yourself with flashcards that you've already made.

However, as long as you do your homework in the way that I've suggested, you will be regularly testing yourself.

Keep it Simple: Focus on One to Three Tools that Work for You

OK, so now I've given you everything I've got. I've laid out all of these study tools so that you have options, because I never want learning to feel like torture or drudgery for you. But please don't feel overwhelmed by all these choices. Using *only one* study tool—for example, perhaps taking notes—could really be all you need to totally transform your learning. Just choose something to do during your Focused Study Sessions that you feel excited to try.

If you find it doesn't work the way you were hoping it would, no worries! You can just try another tool. It's all about what works best for *you* and your learning process. That's what metacognition—thinking about thinking—is all about.

Of course, if you want to go for broke and use all the variations of all seven tools, go for it!

Now, a couple of questions for you:

1. What note-taking strategies or tools have you used up to this point? Feel free to include tools that may not be listed in this guide.

2. What note-taking strategies and tools from this guide do you think you might want to try in the future?

Final Note: Why Memorizing Is Still Important Even Though We Want to Go to Higher Learning Levels

Your parent or mentor has explained to you why it's important not to get stuck at the bottom of the pyramid of learning levels by *only* memorizing. But you might be asking yourself: Why do I have to memorize anything at all if I have the internet at my fingertips? The answer is that we can only think creatively with the information we have in our heads. Memorizing is the foundation of learning. That's why it's at the bottom of the pyramid. Everything rests upon it. So it's extremely valuable to learn to do simple math in your head or to memorize vocabulary words, history dates, or literary terms, for example.

My older daughter is a doctor and a professor. Once she asked a student if it was wise to give pregnant women a drug that acts like adrenaline. She expected him to think hard about it, but instead he just looked it up on the internet and answered, "No." But he couldn't tell her *why* that was the right answer. Later, when he thought about it, he realized it was obvious that a drug that makes blood vessels smaller is not a good idea for a woman carrying a child. If he had taken the time to *memorize* (pyramid level 1) the effects of adrenaline, then he could have *applied* (level 3) that knowledge immediately. He would have realized that, because a pregnant woman's blood vessels need to deliver blood to both herself and the baby, anything that acts like adrenaline would not be good for her. Now let me ask you: Would you rather have a doctor who looks up everything on the internet, focusing on questions of *what* instead of *why*, or a doctor who can think creatively on the spot, quickly add new information to their understanding, and come up with solutions to help you feel better?

If you would prefer the second type of doctor, I hope you will feel inspired to lay the important groundwork of memorizing so that you can eventually have a lot of fun climbing to the very top of Bloom's pyramid of learning. No matter what field you decide to go into—the arts, business, technical fields, law, or any number of other areas—when you've taken the time to memorize the basics, you can start to think creatively. And *that's* when you can start to contribute new and valuable innovations and insights to your field. As you soar, you will be helping humanity meet the challenges of the day.

Keep Handout 6.5 handy as a quick reference of study tools.

How to Find a Tutor

In this guide, I lay out some issues you may want to consider if you need to find a tutor to help your child. It assumes that you have already consulted with your child's teacher and followed their recommendations but still need more support.

To Hire a Tutor, Or Not to Hire a Tutor: That is the Question

The whole point of this book is to minimize the probability that your child will need a tutor. I believe that the majority of people who get tutoring would not need it if they had effective learning strategies. For example, I once worked with an LSU football player who was failing algebra. Although he had a tutor for the class, he couldn't understand her explanations of the subject material. I told him that I would teach him how to be his *own* tutor. After learning the strategies presented in this book, he raised his grade in algebra from an F to a B by making As on all of the remaining tests. So one way of thinking about my entire approach is that I'm teaching people how to be their own tutors.

Having said that, of course I recognize that sometimes hiring a tutor is wise and necessary. Everyone benefits from working with someone who has more expertise than they do. If you are interested in hiring a tutor in order to optimize your child's learning, it's wise to ensure that your child has maximized what they can accomplish independently.

A Range of Different Options

There are many different kinds of tutoring, ranging from no-cost peer tutoring to high-end tutoring for hundreds of dollars an hour. You'll need find the right fit for your child, your family, and your wallet. I've laid out four general options, which all come in two flavors: individual or group. A group can be anywhere from two to fifteen or more students.

- Free tutoring from students or teachers provided by your child's school

- Free tutoring from community groups or local volunteers

- Private tutoring from an independent tutor

- Private tutoring with a company

Clearly Identify Your Needs

Two important questions to ask before beginning your search are:

1. Which subject or subjects does my child need help with?

2. How often do I think my child will need help?

If your child needs help with multiple subjects, then it may be more time- and cost-efficient to find one or two tutors who cover all of those subjects instead of hiring one for each subject. How often your child sees a tutor could range from several times a week to once a semester, although most students meet with their tutors on a weekly basis. Knowing how often your child needs help will enable the tutor candidates to know whether they have the availability to work with your family.

$, $$, or $$$?

Prices for private tutoring can range from $10 to $300 (or more) per hour, depending on where you live and who you hire. Most fees will be somewhere in the range of $30 to $200 per hour. If you know other parents who use tutors, you can get an idea of what the market rate is in your city. An internet search for "[Your city] tutoring companies" will also give you that information. You can see what you can find out just by clicking around, or you can call the first few hits and ask for their rates. With tutoring, as with anything else, you usually get what you pay for, but it's possible to find bargains. It is also possible to pay above-market rate for inferior work.

Ways to Bring Down the Price

Here are some suggestions for finding the lowest cost tutoring you can. Be aware that some of these may carry with them the risk of lowering the tutoring quality.

- Explore free tutoring options with your school's parent association, your local library, or your local government representative. Some free programs have excellent tutors who get great results with their students.

- Look for tutoring flyers at your local college or university from students in the department your child needs help in. This strategy is like getting dental work from a dental school student.

- Ask the tutor candidate or the tutoring company representative whether there is an option for small group tutoring with a lower hourly rate per student.

- Ask the tutor candidate or company rep whether there is an income-based sliding scale. Some tutors and tutoring companies offer rates based on family income.

- Ask whether there is a discount for purchasing, or even committing to, several sessions at once, after an initial session.

- Ask whether a tutoring company might offer a free or discounted first session.

- Negotiate the rate if it's appropriate. See what they can do. (If you are talking to an independent tutor, however, drop any attempt to negotiate if you sense their discomfort.)

- Explore online tutoring options. These can often be cheaper than in-person tutoring. Do an internet search for "online tutoring [subject] [grade level]." You won't need to include the grade level if the subject is something like AP biology.

- See if you can get a friends-and-family rate from someone you know.

- See if it's possible to barter with another parent if you are qualified to tutor a subject. You may also be able to barter as long as the tutor candidate needs whatever skill you are offering, from plumbing or accounting help to guitar or surfing lessons. You never know.

Independent Tutor vs. Tutoring Company

The advantages of hiring an independent tutor include the fact that prices are usually lower (since you're not paying for overhead) and you have a direct relationship with the tutor. The advantages of using a company include quality control: if it's a company with a good reputation, as well as good reviews and testimonials, then it has usually done the work to ensure that tutors are high-quality and reliable. It can also be useful to separate conversations with the tutor about your child's learning from conversations about pricing and commitment. But those aren't reasons to rule out going with an independent tutor. Many tutors prefer working for themselves, so some of the best and most experienced ones will be independent. Each option has its pros and cons.

Where to Start Your Search

Your best option is to go with someone who has been recommended to you by another parent or someone else in your network, as long as that tutor has gotten good results with students who are similar to your child. For example, if your friend recommends a math tutor who usually works with 11th graders, but your child is a 4th grader, then going with an experienced fourth grade math tutor is probably a better option than your friend's recommendation.

A recommendation from your child's teacher or guidance counselor is another great option that you can explore even if you already have someone in mind through word-of-mouth. Find out from the teacher how strong their recommendation is. Is this someone the teacher routinely sends their students to? Or is this a name the teacher is just throwing out there because otherwise they would have no names to offer?

If you ask around and come up empty-handed, and you've exhausted your options at the local university, then it's time to turn to the internet. Searches will likely turn up both in-person and online options. By "in-person," I include tutors who may be working online during the pandemic but who, in non-COVID times, would be meeting your child in person. Each website should feature credible reviews and testimonials. Don't ignore anything that sets off your Spidey senses.

The First Phone Call or Email Exchange

Once you've identified some tutor candidates and prospective tutoring companies, you're ready to reach out. I recommend an initial phone call, rather than email, because there's a lot of information you can get from tone and attitude that might be missing in an email. But there's nothing wrong with digital communication if that's what you're more comfortable with.

When reaching out to independent tutors, be aware that the higher the candidate's fee, the more of their time you can take during that initial exchange without seeming impolite or inconsiderate. Try to do your research before the conversation. Find out what you can about them from the information posted online. The following four sections cover the range of issues you may want to explore during that first conversation.

Credentials, Experience, References, and Results

A candidate's credentials include their education and work history. Try not to be dazzled by fancy schools. It might tell you something about the tutor's intellectual fitness, but it doesn't tell you anything about their ability to help your child excel. One of my students at LSU had to leave school after his father died, but he became so successful at and well-known for helping middle schoolers excel in math that a parent ended up funding the remainder of his education. But for several months he was a college dropout who was, nonetheless, a superstar math tutor. So education doesn't always tell the whole story.

Usually, more years of experience is better than fewer, but that doesn't mean a relatively new tutor can't be wonderful. Plus, they are usually less expensive. If the tutor is independent, then a history working for companies is a good sign. It means they've gone through mandatory trainings and usually have experience working with a range of families. But having a fully independent resume shouldn't be a dealbreaker.

The candidate should be able to offer you two to three references—other families to contact—or testimonials about their previous work. Finally, they should be able to tell you some success stories. Someone who is really on the ball will have facts and figures like what percentage of their students have seen an increase in their grades, or the average improvement that their students see. But keeping and analyzing that information takes time that many of the most successful, and busiest, tutors simply don't have. So hard data should not be a requirement.

Which Subjects Does the Candidate Tutor and How Long Have They Been Doing It?

At some point during the conversation, the candidate should explain how they came to tutor the subject your child needs help in. Sometimes it's obvious: a math major who tutors math, for example. But sometimes tutors who begin in one area branch out to others. My younger daughter began by tutoring biology and chemistry, but by the time she left the industry, she was also tutoring math, English, French, and standardized test prep.

Ideally, you want someone who has been tutoring their subject for a long time and who knows your child's specific school, its teachers, and how its classes work. But that's just the dream scenario; an excellent, or even indispensable, tutor absolutely doesn't need to know all of that information. What you usually *don't* want is someone who is just beginning to branch out into a new subject area. You basically don't want a tutor who is stretching their limits and finding their sea legs with your child. But again, there are exceptions. An extremely talented tutor could do a great job with a subject that is new to them. Plus, if you need a tutor who covers a range of subjects, then you may decide to be more lenient. If you think the tutor will get along well with your child, then it'll probably be fine if they have less experience in an area your child needs slightly less help in.

What is the Candidate's Tutoring Philosophy?

During your initial exchange, the candidate should also share their tutoring philosophy with you. Someone's tutoring philosophy is basically just what they think the tutoring process should involve—what tutoring should *do*. Whether the candidate's philosophy feels right to you depends on what you want for your child. There's a wide spectrum of approaches. At one extreme end, the goal is for your child to get the highest grades by any means necessary. At the other extreme, the goal is for your child to think and learn completely independently. A tutor who prioritizes grades might spend a lot of time spelling out concepts to your child and making them digestible, as well as sharing practical shortcuts like how to plan a five-paragraph essay or problem-solving timesavers like using a calculator for simple arithmetic. On the other hand, a tutor who prioritizes independence might mostly ask questions of your child and demand much more metacognition from them. Both kinds of tutors can work. My ideal tutor would be a combination of the two, with a bigger emphasis on metacognition and intellectual independence.

I'm not suggesting that you should have a long conversation with the candidate about the ins and outs of different educational theories. In fact, the tutor might offer their tutoring philosophy in a single, simple sentence without your even having to ask. Just make sure you're on the same page. And after absorbing the contents of this book, you will be well positioned to judge for yourself whether the candidate works in a way that is consistent with the principles laid out here. You can also always just tell a tutor, "I don't want you to spoon-feed my child. If you have to do some of that initially for their grades to come up, that's okay, but my goal is for them to eventually become independent. I want them to know how to learn the material for themselves."

The Tutor-Student Fit

I'm sure you're familiar with the phenomenon whereby your child, or another child you know, just does not get along with a teacher that a lot of other students adore. That can also happen with tutors. It should be clear after the first session whether the fit is right. My younger daughter was a popular and sought-after tutor in a large competitive metropolitan market, but it just didn't work between her and some students. Eventually, she got into a groove with students who thrived on her intellectually demanding tutoring style and work-hard-play-hard attitude.

To investigate this issue a bit during your initial exchange with the tutor, you can ask whether the tutor has ever worked with students who share traits or circumstances with your child in whatever ways you think are important. Those might include personality, specific concepts they're having trouble with, their school, the teacher of the class they're having trouble in, or a learning disability diagnosis—any characteristics you think are important to mention. This serves two purposes: It gives you information about the tutor's experience, and it gives the tutor a heads-up about your child.

You might also keep an eye out for possible role models. For example, if your child is a girl with an interest in science, math, technology, or engineering, you could consider hiring a woman for her to work with because women are underrepresented in those fields.

Finally, everything could be clicking between you and the candidate except your schedules. The tutor only has availability after 6 p.m., but your child has evening rehearsals almost every night of the week. Unfortunately, you'll need to move on to the next candidate.

Gather Your Thoughts Before You Call

I've given you a lot to think about, but that doesn't mean your initial contact with a prospective tutor or tutoring company has to take longer than five or ten minutes. Figure out what you need, ask a few open-ended questions, let the candidate sell themselves, and then ask any follow-up questions you need to. The more respectful you can be with the tutor, the more the tutor will want to make sure they deliver for you.

After the First Session

After the first session, call the tutor in order to get their impression of where your child is and what they need in order to excel. Checking in with the tutor in a phone call instead of in your front hallway—with your child in eavesdropping range—means that the tutor will feel free to be completely honest with you. Naturally you will also check in with your child to see how they felt about the first session and any questions they may have. If the tutor's estimation of what your child needs feels like a surprise, quickly check with your child's teacher to see if they agree. Once everyone is onboard, you're good to go.

What to Watch Out for in an Ongoing Relationship

Ideally, once you've found a good tutor for your child, their performance will improve and they will eventually become independent. Sometimes, though, there are bumps in the road. Just like in any relationship, everybody puts their best foot forward in the beginning. If you sense something change, or your child's grades start to slip, first check in with your child. If that doesn't solve the mystery, call the tutor and ask if they know what the issue might be. Just making that check-in might be enough to right the ship. If not, start looking for a replacement.

If you are working with a tutor who covers multiple subjects and multiple age groups, there may be a point where your child ages out of their target group. If that situation applies to you, just be prepared for it.

Also be aware that a tutor's rates will typically go up by 3–10% every couple of years. In some markets, raising rates every year is normal and matches the pattern of local rents.

Specialized Tutoring

There are specialized tutoring systems for students who are neurodiverse or have learning disabilities. For example, some tutoring programs for dyslexia use Orton-Gillingham methods.[16] Children's Dyslexia Centers sponsors this kind of tutoring in several states at no cost. Furthermore, there are local companies as well as independent tutors who specialize in working with students with neurodiverse conditions or learning disabilities. This is a vast topic outside the scope of this book, but nowadays there is a lot of helpful information online for parents. Start with the two websites suggested in the Recommended Resources.

Tutor Alternatives

Sometimes, students' challenges go beyond specific subject matter. They might struggle with executive functioning organizational skills, or learning-processing delays and require a professional who can address their particular challenge. Again, start with the two websites in the Recommended Resources section to find information about how you can explore good local options for your child. You can also reach out to your local college or university to see if it offers relevant workshops or training that you or your child can attend. Even though these workshops typically occur in a college setting, many of the concepts or strategies offered can be applied at any educational level.

Hiring Someone to Deliver the Content in This Book

I mentioned in this book's introduction that if you have a difficult relationship with your child you could consider hiring a tutor to deliver the information in this book to them. If you're reading this guide for that purpose, then in your initial conversation with the tutor candidate, just say, "A learning strategist named Saundra McGuire has a book out called

The Parents' Guide to Studying and Learning that teaches parents how to deliver learning strategies to their children. But I don't have the time to work through it. Is that something I could hire you for? To read the book and then have a series of sessions with my child to work through the material?" Tutors of any subject who also work with your child's grade level could be suitable candidates.

Tutor Candidate Checklist

I hope I've given you all the information you need to find a tutor who is a great fit for your family. To conclude this guide, I've compiled a list of questions you can refer to while you're making interview calls:

- Are they in my price range?

- Can I negotiate?

- Is their education and work history satisfactory?

- Are their reputation and references or testimonials satisfactory?

- Is their experience in the relevant subject(s) or area(s) satisfactory? Or are they willing to work through *The Parents' Guide to Studying and Learning* with my child?

- Is their approach to tutoring a good fit?

- Do they have experience with students like my child?

- Are our schedules compatible?

Handout Index by Situation

This appendix is an index of handouts and answer keys organized by different situations that students often find themselves in. It has two parts: (1) urgent situations you may need to address before you lead your child through the *Core Content* (see chapter 12) and (2) situations that should be addressed only after you have gone through the *Core Content* with your child. The situations in the second part are best addressed by the *Core Content* itself. Then the targeted handout recommendations can be effective as follow up.

Unlike a conventional index, Appendix D is not organized alphabetically but rather in order of how common each situation is for students, in my experience.

If your child is currently in crisis and you need to use the first part of the Appendix, then once you have gotten through the urgent situation or crisis, lead your child through the *Core Content* in order to give them the best shot at maintaining and building on their progress.

You don't necessarily need to use *all* of the handouts listed under each section, although you certainly can. Judge what your child needs according to their individual circumstances.

Handout Index Part 1: For Urgent Situations

IF YOUR CHILD IS CURRENTLY IN ACADEMIC CRISIS	
Handout 3.2	What is Metacognition and How Can It Help Me?
Handout 4.5	Bloom's Levels of Learning
Handout 5.1	The Study Cycle
Handout 5.2	Focused Study Sessions
Handout 5.3	The Study Cycle and Focused Study Sessions Combined
Handout 6.2	Using Your Homework to Test Your Understanding
Handout 6.3	Ten Learning Strategies
Handout 6.4	Learning Strategies Worksheet
Handout 6.5	Quick Reference: List of Study Tools
Handout 8.4	How to Figure Out What You Are Actually Supposed to Be Doing
Handout 11.4	Procrastination Busters
See also	*Urgent Exam Preparation/Bringing Up Grades* Section

URGENT EXAM PREPARATION/BRINGING UP GRADES	
Appendix A	Test Preparation Guide
Handout 11.6	Learning Strategies Inventory
See also	*If Your Child is Currently in Academic Crisis* Section

DEALING WITH DEVASTATING FAILURE	
Handout 9.2	Dealing with Setbacks, Mistakes, and Failure
Handout 9.3	Stumbling Blocks or Stepping Stones?
Handout 9.4	Mistakes and Failure Worksheet
Answer Key 9.4A	Answer Key for Select Answers on Mistakes and Failure Worksheet
Handout 9.5	A Process for Dealing with Negative Feedback or Failure
Handout 11.5	Exam Wrappers
Handout 11.8	When Overwhelm Strikes

OVERWHELMED, PARALYZED, OR STUCK	
Handout 8.4	How to Figure Out What You Are Actually Supposed to Be Doing
Handout 11.4	Procrastination Busters
Handout 11.8	When Overwhelm Strikes
Take a Nap!	Take a Break!

Handout Index Part 2: For Situations Best Addressed After You've Gone Through the Core Content

The following handout recommendations make sense once an overall framework has been established by the Core Content (see chapter 12). It's better to spend your time giving your child that framework rather than trying to immediately zero in on these issues. Use these as follow up, as situations arise.

ONGOING EXAM PREPARATION	
Appendix A	Test Preparation Guide
Handout 11.5	Exam Wrappers

MAKING STUDYING MORE EFFICIENT	
Handout 3.2	What is Metacognition and How Can It Help Me?
Handout 3.4	Metacognition Worksheet
Answer Key 3.4A	Answer Key for Metacognition Worksheet
Handout 8.3	How Do You Prefer to Learn? (Worksheet)
Handout 8.4	How to Figure Out What You Are Actually Supposed to Be Doing
Handout 10.1	Study Preferences Worksheet
Handout 10.2	Study Session Checklist
Handout 11.3	Getting the Most Out of a Syllabus
Handout 11.5	Exam Wrappers
Handout 11.7	Strategies and Tools Tracker
Appendix B	Study Tools Guide

PLANNING AND TIME MANAGEMENT	
Handout 10.3	Rocks in a Bucket
Handout 10.4	Filling Out Your Term Calendar
Handout 10.5	Filling Out Your Week Calendar
Handout 10.6	App Detox Worksheet
Handout 11.2	Mapping Out Your Year
Handout 11.3	Getting the Most Out of a Syllabus

STRATEGIZING /FINDING INSPIRATION AND DIRECTION	
Handout 8.2	Worksheet about My Interests and Things I Enjoy Doing
Handout 9.6	Worksheet—Defining Success
Handout 11.1	Worksheet: What Gets You Fired Up Deep Down Inside?

The following handout recommendations are appropriate once the *Core Content* has been delivered.

LOW CONFIDENCE OR OVERCONFIDENCE	
Handout 7.1	Fixed and Growth Mindsets
Handout 7.2	Mindset Worksheet
Handout 8.5	Self-Talk Journaling Worksheet
Handout 8.6	Doing What *You* Can and Letting Go of the Rest (Worksheet)
Handout 9.3	Stumbling Blocks or Stepping Stones?
Handout 10.6	App Detox Worksheet
See also	*Overwhelmed, Paralyzed, or Stuck* Section

GENERAL REFERENCE	
Handout 11.9	Quick Reference List of All Learning Support Resources
Handout 4.5	Bloom's Levels of Learning
Handout 5.3	The Study Cycle and Focused Study Sessions Combined
Handout 6.3	Ten Learning Strategies
Handout 6.4	Learning Strategies Worksheet
Handout 6.5	Quick Reference: List of Study Tools
Appendix A	Test Preparation Guide
Handout 11.5	Exam Wrappers

Sections in Part 1 that are also relevant in Part 2:

Dealing with Devastating Failure

Overwhelmed, Paralyzed, or Stuck

List of Handouts and Answer Keys

Note: The first number in each handout name is the chapter that the handout belongs to.

NAME	TITLE
Handout 3.1	Who is Dr. McGuire and Why Should I Care About What She Says?
Handout 3.2	What is Metacognition and How Can It Help Me?
Handout 3.3	Count the Vowels
Handout 3.4	Metacognition Worksheet
Answer Key 3.4A	Answer Key for Metacognition Worksheet
Handout 4.1	Answering Reflection Questions
Handout 4.2	Other Students' Answers to Reflection Question #1
Handout 4.3	Other Students' Answers to Reflection Question #3
Handout 4.4	Alternative Answers to Reflection Question #3
Handout 4.5	Bloom's Levels of Learning
Handout 4.6	Bloom's Levels of Learning: Goldilocks Edition
Answer Key 4.6A	Answer Key for Bloom's Levels of Learning: Goldilocks Edition
Handout 5.1	The Study Cycle
Handout 5.2	Focused Study Sessions
Handout 5.3	The Study Cycle and Focused Study Sessions Combined
Handout 6.1	Guess the Activity/The Power of Previewing
Handout 6.2	Using Your Homework to Test Your Understanding
Handout 6.3	Ten Learning Strategies
Handout 6.4	Learning Strategies Worksheet
Handout 6.5	Quick Reference: List of Study Tools
Handout 7.1	Fixed and Growth Mindsets
Handout 7.2	Mindset Worksheet
Answer Key 7.2A	Answer Key for Select Questions on Mindset Worksheet

(continued)

NAME	TITLE
Handout 8.1	Worksheet for Parents on Motivation
Handout 8.2	Worksheet about My Interests and Things I Enjoy Doing
Handout 8.3	How Do You Prefer to Learn? (Worksheet)
Handout 8.4	How to Figure Out What You Are Actually Supposed to Be Doing
Handout 8.5	Self-Talk Journaling Worksheet
Handout 8.6	Doing What *You* Can and Letting Go of the Rest (Worksheet)
Handout 9.1	Quick Reference List of Helpful Practices and Attitudes About Failure for Parents
Handout 9.2	Dealing with Setbacks, Mistakes, and Failure
Handout 9.3	Stumbling Blocks or Stepping-Stones?
Handout 9.4	Mistakes and Failure Worksheet
Answer Key 9.4A	Answer Key for Select Answers on Mistakes and Failure Worksheet
Handout 9.5	A Process for Dealing with Negative Feedback or Failure
Handout 9.6	Worksheet—Defining Success
Handout 10.1	Study Preferences Worksheet
Handout 10.2	Study Session Checklist
Handout 10.3	Rocks in a Bucket
Handout 10.4	Filling Out Your Term Calendar
Handout 10.5	Filling Out Your Week Calendar
Handout 10.6	App Detox Worksheet
Handout 10.7	Quiz: Saying No, Setting Boundaries, and Protecting Your Time
Handout 11.1	Worksheet: What Gets You Fired Up Deep Down Inside?
Handout 11.2	Mapping Out Your Year
Handout 11.3	Getting the Most out of a Syllabus
Handout 11.4	Procrastination Busters
Handout 11.5	Exam Wrappers
Handout 11.6	Learning Strategies Inventory
Handout 11.7	Strategies and Tools Tracker
Handout 11.8	When Overwhelm Strikes
Handout 11.9	Quick Reference List of All Learning Support Resources
Handout 12.1	Core Content
Handout 12.2	Additional Content
Handout 12.3	Scheduling Your Strategies—Presentation Sessions and Other Check-Ins
Handout 12.4	Setting Clear Expectations for the Year
Appendix A	Test Preparation Guide
Appendix B	Study Tools Guide

Acknowledgments

Producing this book has been an exciting venture for me. First, I am thrilled to deliver to parents what I've learned over the past twenty years about teaching students how to learn. Second, this project has given me the opportunity to reflect upon what a joyful process it has been to accumulate the information, experience, and perspectives that inform this book and its online supplements. I have had the pleasure and privilege of collaborating with and learning from countless individuals over the course of my career and therefore have many, many people to thank for their assistance.

First and foremost, I must thank my dear friend and colleague, Sarah Baird, for introducing me to the idea that students who were failing classes could be transformed into students who excel at the highest levels if only they used specific learning strategies. And she showed me exactly how to teach them those strategies! I also want to thank my colleagues at the LSU Center for Academic Success (CAS) upon whose work many of the ideas and strategies in the book are based. Although I initially taught the strategies to college and professional school students, over the years I worked with many high school students who experienced similar improvements. I want to thank those parents who allowed me to work with their children, and who reinforced the concepts, ideas, and strategies I had introduced to them, in order to ensure that their children's gains in learning would be sustained.

Most sincere thanks to Dan Solomon, our publisher, for having the vision that a version of *Teach Students How to Learn* for parents would allow many more students to benefit from this information. His enthusiasm and indefatigable support have been essential. I also extend heartfelt gratitude to our executive editor, Anja Schmidt, who expertly guided us in crafting a polished manuscript that would be most impactful for our readers. Sincere thanks also go to our copyeditor, Sabrina Detlef, for offering countless suggestions that made a sizeable difference to the quality of the book. Kathleen Dyson also deserves enthusiastic acknowledgement for her masterful design of the book, its cover art, and the online supplements.

I am extremely grateful that my friend and former LSU colleague Dr. Jim McCoy, Vice President of Enrollment Management at Salem College, readily agreed to write the foreword for this book. As a college admissions executive with decades of experience, he has deep insight into the range of learning skills required for success after high school, and I am honored to have his endorsement.

The three expert readers of the manuscript, Sarah Baird, Dr. Eric Kaldor, and Dr. Algernon Kelley provided valuable feedback that resulted in meaningful improvements in the content and the tone of the book. I am most grateful that all of our readers took the time to carefully and thoughtfully read the manuscript and offer their impressions, reactions, and suggestions.

Having been born into a family of educators is perhaps the greatest, most fundamental blessing of my life. My grandmother, Mrs. Effie Jane Gordon Yancy, and my parents, Mr. and Mrs. Robert (Delsie) Yancy, Jr., taught me and my siblings how to be successful students even before many of the concepts in this book had been formally studied. Special thanks also go to my siblings, Robert Yancy III, Dr. Eric A Yancy, and Annette L. Yancy. We formed a small learning community, led by our parents, and experienced some of the strategies put forth here.

Throughout five decades of marriage, my husband Dr. Stephen C. McGuire has provided steadfast and constant support, encouragement, guidance, and inspiration. He is the love of my life, and I give gratitude for the journey we have traveled together. I also offer sincere thanks to our daughters Dr. Carla McGuire Davis and Dr. Stephanie McGuire and to our grandchildren Joshua, Ruth, Daniel, and Joseph Davis. They have all been cheerful subjects as I investigated the ways in which many of the strategies presented here could meet their learning challenges.

I have no words to express my gratitude for my co-author and daughter Dr. Stephanie McGuire, without whom this book would not exist. In addition to creating most of the text for this book, she spent untold hours researching information, designing information delivery systems, and consulting subject-matter experts. In addition to those I have already thanked, she would like to thank Nicolai von Neudeck for socio-technical systems consulting and unwavering support during the writing process. She also thanks Mr. von Neudeck, Dr. Eric Kaldor, and Dr. Holly Swanson for helping her understand the differences between the way natural scientists and social scientists interpret the world. Amy Cowan, Mark McNeill, Audrey Mey, and Gabriella Callender also deserve heartfelt thanks for much needed support. Especially deep gratitude goes to all of the teachers, coaches, and therapists, and psychology or performance professionals she has had the privilege to learn from in her life. Functional nutritionist Karen Kennedy, CN, IFNCP, generously gave her time and provided invaluable information and recommendations. Several consultants also offered indispensable advice about the diagrams in Appendix B: Dr. Thomas Durant, Jr., Mr. Lorenzo Foster, Ms. Emily Halphen, Ms. Stephanie H. Kurtz, Dr. Mary Jo Ondrechen, Ms. Susan Saale, and Dr. E. William Wischusen. Finally, Stephanie would like to extend her own thanks to Anja Schmidt; working with Ms. Schmidt was not only a privilege but a peak professional experience.

If there is anyone we have left out, we offer our profuse apologies. Please know that we have deep gratitude for you. It takes a village to raise a child and also to produce a book! We owe a debt of gratitude to everyone who played a part in *The Parents' Guide to Studying and Learning*.

References

Aguilar, Lauren, Greg Walton, and Carl Wieman. "Psychological Insights for Improved Physics Teaching." *Physics Today* 67 (2014): 43–49.

Ambrose, Susan A., Michael W. Bridges, Michele DiPietro, Marsha C. Lovett, and Marie K. Norman. *How Learning Works: Seven Research-Based Principles for Smart Teaching.* San Francisco, CA: Jossey-Bass, 2010.

Anderson, Lorin, David Krathwohl, Peter Airasian, Kathleen Cruikshank, Richard Mayer, Paul Pintrich, James Raths, and Merlin Wittrock. *A Taxonomy of Learning, Teaching, and Assessing: A Revision of Bloom's Taxonomy of Educational Objectives.* New York: Longman, 2001.

Breines, Juliana G., and Serena Chen. "Self-Compassion Increases Self-Improvement Motivation." *Personality and Social Psychology Bulletin* 38, no. 9 (2012): 1133–1143.

Bloom, Benjamin S., Max D. Englehart, Edward J. Furst, Walker H. Hill, and David R. Krathwohl. *Taxonomy of Educational Objectives: The Classification of Educational Goals.* New York: McKay, 1956.

Dweck, Carol S. *Mindset: The New Psychology of Success.* New York: Random House, 2006.

ESPN. "Richard Jefferson Breaks Down the Cavs' 3-1 Comeback in the 2016 NBA Finals, Highlights with Omar," YouTube video, April 2, 2020, https://www.youtube.com/watch?v=u1jwjlq2pA4

Faber, Adele, and Elaine Mazlish. *How to Talk So Kids Will Listen & Listen So Kids Will Talk.* New York: Perennial Currents, 2004.

Gabriel, Kathleen F. *Teaching Unprepared Students.* Sterling, VA: Stylus Publishing, 2008.

Hillman, Charles, Matthew B. Pontifex, Lauren B. Raine, Darla Castelli, Eric E. Hall, and Arthur F. Kramer. "The Effect of Acute Treadmill Walking on Cognitive Control and Academic Achievement in Preadolescent Children." *Neuroscience* 159, no. 3 (2009): 1044–54.

Hopper, Carolyn H. *Practicing College Learning Strategies.* Boston, MA: Wadsworth, 2013.

Howie, Erin K., Jeffrey Schatz, and Russell R. Pate. "Acute Effects of Classroom Exercise Breaks on Executive Function and Math Performance: A Dose-Response Study." *Research Quarterly for Exercise and Sport* 86, no. 3 (2015): 217–24.

Lovett, Marsha C. "Make Exams Worth More Than the Grade: Using Exam Wrappers to Promote Metacognition." In *Using Reflection and Metacognition to Improve Student Learning*, Matthew Kaplan, Naomi Silver, Danielle Lavaque-Manty, and Deborah Meizlish, 18–52. Sterling, VA: Stylus Publishing, 2013.

Ludyga, Sebastian, Markus Gerber, Keita Kamijo, Serge Brand, and Uwe Pühse. "The Effects of a School-Based Exercise Program on Neurophysiological Indices of Working Memory Operations in Adolescents." *The Journal of Science and Medicine in Sport* 21, no. 8 (2018): 833–838.

McGuire, Saundra Yancy. *Teach Students How to Learn: Strategies You Can Incorporate into Any Course to Improve Student Metacognition, Study Skills, and Motivation.* Sterling, VA: Stylus Publishing, 2015.

McGuire, Saundra Yancy. *Teach Yourself How to Learn: Strategies You Can Use to Ace Any Course at Any Level.* Sterling, VA: Stylus Publishing, 2018.

Neff, Kristin D., Phoebe Long, Marissa C. Knox, Oliver Davidson, Ashley Kuchar, Andrew Costigan, Zachary Williamson, Nicolas Rohleder, István Tóth-Király, and Juliana G. Breines. "The Forest and the Trees: Examining the Association of Self-Compassion and its Positive and Negative Components with Psychological Functioning." *Self and Identity* 17, no. 6 (2018): 627–645.

Pontifex, Matthew B., Brian J. Saliba, Lauren B. Raine, Daniel L. Picchietti, and Charles H. Hillman. "Exercise Improves Behavioral, Neurocognitive, and Scholastic Performance in Children with Attention-Deficit/Hyperactivity Disorder." *The Journal of Pediatrics* 162, no. 3 (2013): 543–551.

Raine, Lauren B., Shih-Chun Kao, Dominika Pindus, Daniel R. Westfall, Tatsuya T. Shigeta, Nicole Logan, Cristina Cadenas-Sanchez, Jane Li, Eric S. Drollette, Matthew B. Pontifex, Naiman A. Khan, Arthur F. Kramer, and Charles H. Hillman. "A Large-Scale Reanalysis of Childhood Fitness and Inhibitory Control." *Journal of Cognitive Enhancement* 2, no. 2 (2018): 170–192.

Shields, Grant S., Wesley G. Moons, and George M. Slavich. "Better Executive Function Under Stress Mitigates the Effects of Recent Life Stress Exposure on Health in Young Adults." *Stress* 20, no. 1 (2017): 75–85.

Stevenson, Harold W., and James W. Stigler. *The Learning Gap: Why Our Schools are Failing and What We Can Learn from Japanese and Chinese Education.* New York: Summit Books, 1992.

Underwood, Paul L. "Are You Overpraising Your Child?" *New York Times.* August 13, 2020. https://www.nytimes.com/2020/08/13/parenting/praising-children.html

Uttal, David H. "Beliefs about Genetic Influences on Mathematics Achievement: A Cross-Cultural Comparison." *Genetica* 99 (1997): 165–172.

Wong, Kristen. "Why Self-Compassion Beats Self-Confidence." *New York Times.* December 28, 2017. https://www.nytimes.com/2017/12/28/smarter-living/why-self-compassion-beats-self-confidence.html

Yeager, David Scott, Valerie Purdie-Vaughns, Julio Garcia, Nancy Apfel, Patti Brzustoski, Allison Master, William T. Hessert, Matthew E. Williams, and Geoffrey L. Cohen. "Breaking the Cycle of Mistrust: Wise Interventions to Provide Critical Feedback Across the Racial Divide." *Journal of Experimental Psychology: General,* 143, no. 2 (2013): 804–824.

Zhao, Ningfeng, Jeffrey G. Wardeska, Saundra Y. McGuire, and Elzbieta Cook. "Metacognition: An Effective Tool to Promote Success in College Science Learning." *Journal of College Science Teaching* 43, no. 4 (2014): 48–54.

Notes

1. Where appropriate, names may have been changed to protect identities.

2. Although I use the term *metacognition* in a way that is easier for students to understand, it also has a rigorous and evolving definition in the educational research literature. I said it this way in my first book: "I purposely blur the distinction between metacognition, learning strategies, and study skills because I am most interested in students' successful application of those tools working in concert." *Teach Students How to Learn*, 15.

3. The academic name for what I'm describing here is Bloom's Taxonomy (Benjamin S. Bloom et al., *Taxonomy of Educational Objectives*; Englehart, Furst, Hill, & Krathwohl, 1956; and Lorin Anderson et al., *A Taxonomy of Learning, Teaching, and Assessing*) but in this book I'll call it Bloom's Levels of Learning. See page 42 of *Teach Students How to Learn*, for more information about the way I (and many others) use Bloom's, and how that usage may differ from other educators' usage.

4. This chapter is based on the work of Stanford psychologist Carol S. Dweck. In recent years, a vigorous discussion about the accuracy of her claims has arisen, with some researchers calling them into question and others pushing back on those criticisms. However, those disagreements are about whether students' mindsets alone can change their performance outcomes. Those controversies are irrelevant to "mindset" as I use it, in conjunction with learning strategies, study tools, the Study Cycle, and Focused Study Sessions. My system uses mindset to motivate students to change their behavior and make more effort. There is universal agreement that more effort and better performance are linked.

5. Shenk, D. (2010) The genius in all of us: Why everything you've been told about genetics, talent, and IQ is wrong. NYC Doubleday.

6. David Scott Yeager et al., "Breaking the Cycle of Mistrust."

7. Susan A. Ambrose et al., How Learning Works.

8. Kathleen F. Gabriel, Teaching Unprepared Students.

9. Underwood, Paul L. "Are You Overpraising Your Child?" New York Times. August 13, 2020. https://www.nytimes.com/2020/08/13/parenting/praising-children.html

10. Lauren Aguilar, Greg Walton, and Carl Wieman, "Psychological Insights for Improved Physics Teaching."

11. Adele Faber and Elaine Mazlish, How to Talk So Kids Will Listen.

12. Kristin D. Neff et al., "The Forest and the Trees."

13. Kristen Wong, "Why Self-Compassion Beats Self-Confidence."

14. Juliana G. Breines and Serena Chen, "Self-Compassion Increases Self-Improvement Motivation," 1133–1134.

15. Charles Hillman et al., "The Effect of Acute Treadmill Walking on Cognitive Control"; Erin K. Howie, Jeffrey Schatz, and Russell R. Pate, "Acute Effects of Classroom Exercise Breaks"; Ludya et al. (2018); Matthew B. Pontifex et al., "Exercise Improves Behavioral, Neurocognitive, and Scholastic Performance"; Lauren B. Raine et al., "A Large-Scale Reanalysis of Childhood Fitness and Inhibitory Control"; and Grant S. Shields, Wesley G. Moons, and George M. Slavich, "Better Executive Function Under Stress."

16. Ritchey, K.D.; Goeke, J.L. (2006). "Orton-Gillingham and Orton-Gillingham Based Reading Instruction: A Review of the Literature". *The Journal of Special Education*. 40 (3): 171–183.

Recommended Resources

BOOKS ON LEARNING

Brown, Peter C., Henry L. Roediger III, and Mark A. McDaniel. *Make It Stick: The Science of Successful Learning.* Cambridge, MA: Harvard University Press, 2014.

Doyle, Terry and Todd Zakrajsek. *The New Science of Learning: How to Learn in Harmony with Your Brain.* Sterling, VA: Stylus, 2013.

Dweck, Carol. *Mindset: The New Psychology of Success.* New York: Random House, 2006.

Kuder, S. Jay, Amy Accardo, and John Woodruff. *College Success for Students on the Autism Spectrum: A Neurodiversity Perspective.* Sterling, VA: Stylus, 2021.

McGuire, Saundra Yancy. *Teach Students How to Learn: Strategies You Can Incorporate into Any Course to Improve Student Metacognition, Study Skills, and Motivation.* Sterling, VA: Stylus Publishing, 2015.

McGuire, Saundra Yancy. *Teach Yourself How to Learn: Strategies You Can Use to Ace Any Course at Any Level.* Sterling, VA: Stylus Publishing, 2018.

Interested readers can also see the Reference section for more.

BOOKS ON NUTRITION AND SLEEP

Antine, Stacey. *Appetite for Life.* HarperOne, 2012.

Although this book is for youth up to the age of 15, it includes many recipes suitable for older teens and adults. Recommended by a functional nutritionist.

Lair, Cynthia. *Feeding the Young Athlete: Sports Nutrition Made Easy for Players, Parents, and Coaches.* San Francisco, CA: Readers to Eaters, 2012.

Although this book is about feeding athletes, the recipes and nutritional principles are suitable for any teen. Recommended by a functional nutritionist.

Walker, Matthew. *Why We Sleep.* Harlow, England: Penguin Books, 2018.

WEBSITES

National Center for Learning Disabilities

This website is a great place to start when you are trying to determine whether your child may have a learning disability and what steps to take next. If you do an internet search for "National Center for Learning Disabilities checklist," you will find a tool that asks you a series of questions about your child and then makes some recommendations. Find the page with the button "Start the checklist" to use this tool.

National Institute of Child Health and Human Development

This is a .gov website with a great deal of information about childhood development, mental health, learning disabilities in general, and specific learning disabilities.

MyStudyLife

This website and its companion app have been recommended by an executive functioning coach to help with organizational skills.

Khan Academy

This website is a free resource provided by a nonprofit organization with well-designed online courses and supplemental academic help. High schoolers are one of this organization's target groups.

About the Authors

Saundra Yancy McGuire, PhD is an internationally acclaimed learning specialist who has been teaching students strategies for improving their learning for more than fifty years. She was named a 2022 Louisiana Legend by Louisiana Public Broadcasting for her numerous national awards. In 2007, she was recognized for excellence in mentoring with a Presidential Award presented in a White House Oval Office Ceremony. She is also an elected Fellow of the American Association for the Advancement of Science (2011), the American Chemical Society (2010), and the Council of Learning Assistance and Developmental Education Associations (2012). In 2013 she retired as Assistant Vice Chancellor and Professor of Chemistry at Louisiana State University, and in 2017 she was inducted into the LSU College of Science Hall of Distinction. She is now Professor Emerita of Chemistry and Director Emerita of the LSU Center for Academic Success, which was recognized by the National College Learning Center Association as the nation's most outstanding learning center in 2004 and is currently designated as a national Learning Center of Excellence. Saundra has presented her widely acclaimed learning strategies workshops at more than 500 institutions in forty-seven states and thirteen countries. She received her B.S. degree, magna cum laude, from Southern University in Baton Rouge, LA, her Master's degree from Cornell University, and her Ph.D. from the University of Tennessee at Knoxville, where she received the Chancellor's Citation for Exceptional Professional Promise. She is married to Physics Professor Emeritus Stephen C. McGuire, and they are the parents of Dr. Carla McGuire Davis and Dr. Stephanie McGuire and the doting grandparents of Joshua, Ruth, Daniel, and Joseph Davis.

Stephanie McGuire holds a bachelor's degree in biology from Massachusetts Institute of Technology, master's and doctoral degrees in neuroscience from the University of Oxford, and a master's degree in opera performance from the Longy Conservatory. She attended Oxford on a Marshall scholarship and received a graduate fellowship from the National Science Foundation. Partly as a result of long and stimulating conversations with her mother about pedagogy and learning strategies, Stephanie became a highly sought-after private academic tutor in the New York City area where she lived for ten years. By coauthoring this book, she is delighted to contribute to Dr. Saundra McGuire's admirable and revolutionary mission to make all students expert learners. Since graduating from conservatory, Stephanie has enjoyed forging a successful career as a classical mezzo-soprano. She has performed with the New York City Opera at Lincoln Center, with the Boston POPS Orchestra in Symphony Hall, and several times at Carnegie Hall. She now lives in Berlin.